WINNING COVER LETTERS

CAREER COACH

WINNING COVER LETTERS

ROBIN RYAN

John Wiley & Sons, Inc.

New York • Chichester • Weinheim • Brisbane • Singapore • Toronto

Copyright © 1997 by Robin Ryan
Published by John Wiley & Sons, Inc.

ISBN: 0-471-19063-2

Printed in the United States of America
10 9 8 7 6 5 4 3 2 1

For my husband Steven

and

some special friends
who all make living worthwhile:
Cindy, Wendy, Martha, and Peggy

CONTENTS

ACKNOWLEDGMENTS

There would be no book if it weren't for all the clients and seminar participants who have used The Power Impact Technique and found it to be such a successful tool. I owe a debt of thanks to the many clients whose stories you'll read. They generously offered insights and hoped their success might inspire others.

So many employers offered their expertise to aid me in this book. I thank everyone who took the time to answer our survey and call, fax, or write me with their insights and observations.

The book improved because Steve Ryan, Scott Thompson, Lisa O'Toole, and Tracy White read the manuscript and offered terrific suggestions on how to make it better.

I'm fortunate to have the best agent in the world—Shelley Roth. I'm grateful for all her efforts and support. I own a *big* thank-you to Mike Hamilton, my editor at Wiley and everyone else there who helped me with this book. Additionally I want to thank Chris Furry and her team for all they did to make this book look terrific.

Dawnie Thompson is owed a mountain of thanks for all her administrative efforts—typing and formatting each page—plus her ongoing support and encouragement that my work makes an important difference in many people's lives.

WINNING COVER LETTERS

A GREAT COVER LETTER IS A KEY ELEMENT IN LANDING THE PERFECT JOB

"I got the job! I can't believe it—I *got* the *job!* I only sent out this one resumé and cover letter—and I got it!" Mary was ecstatic as she called to tell me her dream had come true. "Four hundred and five people applied and they picked me—*me!*" Her elation over landing a great new job was passionate. Cindy, another client, called to say: "They hired me. This is a dream job—more money, better hours. It's perfect. I knew I needed to write a good resumé and cover letter. All it took was one. I never sent another. From just that first one, I got the call. I start in two weeks. I would never have believed it could be this easy. This will change my whole life. After 20 years, I'm finally moving on to the perfect job for me. Hard to believe, but it's true."

Phone calls, letters, notes—they all say the same thing: "I got the job!" "Thank you for your help, that *cover letter* did the trick. I've got the interview." No one was more thrilled than Sam. He sent me an expensive bouquet of flowers with a letter that said: "No one had even looked at me before I worked with you. Taking three years off from my career was proving to be the professional suicide my friends warned me it would be; but you helped me put together a strategy, reworked my resumé, and improved my cover letters. You had me focus on what I had accomplished—to really market my strengths and talents. I've just landed a senior management position my colleagues will be envious of."

These clients, like all the others in this book, had great success using The Power Impact Technique to write their cover letters. That is the technique you'll learn in the upcoming pages to ensure you put your absolute best on paper. These letters made the difference.

96% of the hiring managers surveyed preferred The Power Impact Technique to write a cover letter.

Extensive research was conducted to offer you *the most effective* job hunting techniques available. An exclusive hiring managers' survey was conducted so you can learn exactly *what* employers want when they hire. Successful cover letters that real people used to land their dream jobs are included; and most important, you'll learn The Power Impact Technique to write the best cover letter possible.

The Importance of Cover Letters

The cover letter is the very first thing the employer sees when you apply for a job. In the course of conducting research to write this book, I confirmed one very important fact—hiring managers and personnel people all stressed the need to write a great cover letter that is targeted to their needs. The candidates who stood out to employers used short but powerful evidence as they wrote sentence after sentence on their past achievements and the talents and contributions they'd bring to the new employer. Your letters must concisely outline your talents and abilities to meet the employer's specific job needs. You'll be able to do that with ease once you start using The Power Impact Technique.

To learn exactly what employers wanted, I developed a survey about cover letters that was sent to 600 hiring managers. The results, coupled with other research based on years of working with career counseling clients, plus my own extensive hiring background, is what formulated the recommendations you'll learn using this book. A significant distinction from other books is that I conducted a hiring survey exclusively for this book. The pages are laced with the results.

Hiring managers will be advising you on what impresses them in a cover letter and what makes them dismiss a candidate in less than 10 seconds.

Human resources manager Barbara Baker tells us: "In my experience I've hired over 1,200 people. I've seen so many mistakes—too long, too short, general, nonspecific content, some even state the reasons they were fired. It boils down to this—a simple, direct letter that mentions how their skills relate to performing the position applied for."

Sounds simple, doesn't it? Yet as we received our hiring surveys back from employers all over the country, we kept hearing the same message:

Most people write a terrible cover letter, so they never get an interview and they never land the job.

Our Hiring Managers' Survey Results

Little research has been done on cover letters. One study confirmed that indeed cover letters *are* important. I felt it was warranted to create a survey to get more specifics about the effectiveness (or lack thereof) from a job candidate's cover letter. I wanted to learn what hiring managers considered the biggest mistakes people make and also what were the best ways to impress them and get the employer's attention.

Therefore, we sent our hiring survey to a random sampling of 600 human resource managers, CEOs, vice presidents, senior executives, and recruiters to determine their preferences. Of these, 38% were in human resources and the other 62% were hiring managers. Everyone in the study had done extensive and recent hiring. Almost all of the HR managers had hired over 200 people, some as many as 1,000. They worked in all different fields: manufacturing, nonprofits, state and federal governments, education, retail, healthcare, service and high tech, to cite a few. Our managers held positions as program directors, vice presidents, senior management, presidents, and CEOs. They had, on average, hired 80 people each. Most senior executives and those at large organizations typically had hired over 100 managers and professionals for their organization.

The survey targeted professional, executive, and managerial positions, with a few questions targeted toward staff jobs. These hiring managers (the person who decides if you get the job) worked for the Fortune 500—some of the best and most prominent companies and organizations in the United States. Others were employed with medium-sized or smaller companies. We covered a wide range of fields and every state in the union to get the real facts on what it takes to get hired today.

The conclusions from this hiring survey will be revealed as you use this book to land your perfect job:

✔ Cover letters are important and necessary.

✔ A good cover can sail to the top of the stack and get an interview. Likewise, a terrific candidate with a general letter will go unnoticed in a stack of hundreds of others vying for the opportunity.

✔ Cover letters serve as a sample of your communication skills.

✔ Succinct points that clearly outline the abilities to perform the needed tasks of the job get noticed.

✔ Of the employers surveyed, 96% selected The Power Impact Technique as their preferred way to write a letter.

In addition to this survey, let me summarize my background. I've been a career counselor for over 15 years. Helping people find good jobs is my passion—the mission that drives my life. I've personally hired over 300 people and teach seminars on hiring to employers. I'm constantly working with job hunters, having seen tens of thousands of participants in my job search seminars. In addition, I conduct hundreds of career counseling sessions with individual clients every year. The reason I wrote this book is for one reason and one reason only: The Power Impact Technique enables job hunters to write more effective cover letters that employers notice and respond to. My clients have proved this over and over again, day after day.

We asked our hiring managers in the survey what was the best way to write a cover letter—*96% selected The Power Impact Technique.* That's the best reason I can give you to use this book—it works! Every cover letter in this book is that of a client I've coached with who got the interview and, in most cases, went on to land a terrific job.

Why Use The Power Impact Technique™?

Employers told us:

"Clearly tell me how you can do the job."　　　　　　*—CEO*

"Show me how you used your skills."　　　*—Department manager*

"What contributions did you make before."　　　*—Vice president*

"Tell me what you can offer my company that makes you special."　　　*—President*

"Tell me why should I select you for an interview."
　　　　　　　　　—Human resource manager

"Be specific."　　　　　　　　*—Personnel director*

"Give clear examples of past success."　　　*—Executive director*

"Relate your background to the job's needs and articulate how you'll meet them."　　　*—Senior vice president*

All these employers are stating exactly how to impress them and get their attention.

I developed The Power Impact Technique over a dozen years ago to help myself get a job. The job market was so competitive, and starting out each letter saying "I'm applying for the job I saw in Sunday's paper" was getting me nowhere. So I created a new writing style. My letter opened with a powerful first sentence that quickly demonstrated to the employer the background and skills I'd bring to the job. My letters began to sail to the top: While hundreds of others missed out, I got the employer's all-important phone call to come in for an interview.

It worked so well for me I started sharing this technique with friends. In 1986, I started leading job search seminars and began teaching this technique to job hunters. I received tremendous positive feedback that this technique was an easy-to-use formula that saved people hours and hours of time spent writing ineffective letters employers never noticed.

Just as I've taught others over the years, now I'll show you how to analyze a job, target a special company, and portray your top strengths using this technique. You'll read employers' comments and insights that will aid you in getting hired *faster* as you look for a new and better job.

You'll find that The Power Impact Technique is both easy-to-use and highly effective to write cover letters employers notice.

You won't find tricks, gimmicks, or shenanigans that don't work. You'll find only letters with a proven success record that you'll get from my years of research on hiring, plus specific employer insights that will enable you to succeed in no time.

Acknowledged Difficulties in Getting Employer's Attention

If you've been in the job market for more than five minutes lately, you'll be the first one to admit it's a challenging time. The competition for each job can draw hundreds of probable candidates . . . *hundreds.* Employers told us the cover letter gets only a few seconds' glance unless, as HR manager Tim Smith said, "I see the skills jumping off the page. It's really hard to read boring letter after boring letter. Or those bragging ones claiming they can do the job. It's rare to break out of the monotony and find a person who took some extra time and crafted a letter that clearly addressed the job's needs as they outlined their abilities and skills. Those rare letters—I notice. Usually those are the ones I hire." Tim works for one of the Fortune 500 companies where they get over 500 letters every week. As he said, "I've seen it all."

Our hiring survey results determined that cover letters receive only a 10-second glance during the initial reading by employers.

You have *only seconds* to capture the employer's attention and keep him or her reading. Good jobs (those that are interesting and pay well) are hard to find. You *must* put together the best possible package to advertise your skills. The bottom line is that *the cover letter is the first thing an employer sees. It must be great!* No ifs, ands, or buts. You need to be better than the competition—you must outsmart them. And you will when you start writing The Power Impact Technique letters.

A Guarantee

This book will improve your ability to write better cover letters. You'll gain insight into what employers are really looking for. Certainly a cover letter alone doesn't get you hired. Rather, it's the letter-writing process you'll learn that means the difference between landing the job or just getting left in the stack. This process includes the job analysis, the insights from the hiring manager's perspective, developing succinct sound bites on your skills, and summarizing the results and contributions you make. This is what you'll be learning and carrying through on your resumé and throughout your interview.

You will read dozens of proven, market-tested letters and success stories that clearly illustrate how to apply The Power Impact Technique yourself. You'll save time and effort while you zero in on a great job you are qualified for with succinct evidence and statements that cause employers to start calling you!

What's Ahead

You'll learn a huge amount of information and insight once you've read through the 42 mistakes employers pointed out that you *must avoid* to get hired!

You'll see examples of people just like you—others who faced the challenge, the fears, and the rejections. The result: They are now enjoying terrific jobs. You'll benefit from reading their stories and seeing exactly how we wrote their cover letters. These cover letters are the exact ones they used—only their names have been changed to ensure their confidentiality. Most books just give samples, but samples only encourage you to copy and not apply the writing skill. That's the difference *Winning Cover Letters* makes. You'll learn The Power Impact Technique. It's an easy writing formula that you'll be able to apply and use to improve your cover letters and your success.

Let's get started. A better job is out there, just waiting for you to find it.

COVER LETTER MISTAKES
HIRING MANAGERS
SAY TO AVOID

"The best way for someone to impress us is to address how all of the qualifications in the opening will be met by the candidate. Spell it out for me succinctly!" says Kirk Beyer, a human resources director.

Concise evidence—that's what employers want. You must tell them exactly how you can do the job! The Power Impact Technique that I'm going to teach you in this book will show you exactly how to write cover letters that hiring managers such as Kirk love to receive. They are specific. They are concise. They address the employer's needs and focus the entire letter on demonstrating skills, experiences, and past accomplishments to excel at the job the employer needs done.

To provide you with the very best strategic advantage possible, I decided to conduct a massive survey to underscore the best ways to write a cover letter and find a job. Little research has been done on cover letters prior to this book. One recent survey's purpose was to determine whether cover letters were even needed at all. The results: Surprisingly, 60% of the 1,000 employers surveyed stated cover letters were "*as important as or more important*" than resumés. That was important, significant data— every resumé needs to have a cover letter. But I wanted more facts on what impresses employers and facts on what people do wrong. So I developed a new survey that asked those questions. We sent 600 surveys to human resource managers, CEOs, VPs, managers, executive recruiters, and department heads—a random cross-sampling nationwide. I wanted people who make hiring decisions from various fields and industries as well as different geographical locations for an accurate representation. I've based this book on the results of this survey, the years of experience I have working with hundreds of employers plus thousands of job hunters, and my own hiring experience. (I've hired over 300 people myself.) I teach hiring seminars to employers and have also worked with them on the selection process. But my first love has always been coaching job hunters like you to find better jobs. This chapter is the result of significant new research done specifically for this book to help you.

I've quoted employers and identified their names, titles, and organizations where we had been given permission to include all three. Several preferred their company names not be identified, so those messages include only name, title, or general company description. These employers' insights will be of significant value to you as you read this book. I think you'll find it to be a very informative and insightful process to hear what these employers told us. The most important result was the endorsement of the effectiveness of The Power Impact Technique. You'll see firsthand evidence of how persuasive a good letter can be.

Additionally, employers were quite verbal about mistakes they often see that cause job hunters to fail. I think a great deal can be learned by understanding more about the hiring process. In this chapter, you'll get a more accurate picture of how employers think and what they value.

We found 42 major errors that you need to avoid as you seek a new position. These are errors that prevented people from getting hired. I suggest you carefully read through this section—you'll learn a great deal.

The following errors are based on what hiring managers told me.

Mistakes You Should Not Make

1 Don't Start Your Letter with: "I'm Applying for the Job I Saw in Sunday's Newspaper"

Imagine yourself with 200 resumés to sort through and 195 start their cover letter this way: "I'm applying for the job I saw in Sunday's paper." We gave our hiring managers several choices of openings for cover letters—*96%* selected The Power Impact Technique—the very technique you'll learn to use in this book. This technique includes a strong opening sentence. It shows you how to address the requested criteria as you identify the job an employer needs done and your ability to excel in performing it. Sue Carroll, executive vice president at Westar Insurance Managers, recommends: "Start your letter with your 'closing statement.' " Pete DeBottis, school district administrator, echoes the same sentiment. He states: "Use an opening paragraph that tells me what you feel you can do to fill the position I have available."

 **2** Forget Form Letters

Victor, a CEO in the healthcare industry, said a major mistake is mailing in a letter that is like a form letter being sent to every prospective employer. Several other employers agreed. In the haste to get the resumé in the mail, the applicant uses the one letter he or she created and does not adapt it to the specifications of each different opening. Job hunters overlook the importance of targeting each and every letter to address that employer's specific needs and requirements. That's why so many candidates get overlooked. Once you offer solid facts, skills, and abilities as evidence of how well you can do the job, your success with potential employers will improve dramatically.

3 Misspelled Words Are Killers

So many employers in our survey responded that nothing stops them faster in their tracks than spelling errors. I repeatedly was told, "I stop reading when I see spelling mistakes." Proofread, proofread, and use a dictionary—so your letters will be perfect.

4 Spellcheckers Miss the Word Meanings

I was never happier than the day I began to use the computer's spellchecker function. Unfortunately, spellcheckers correct misspellings but they don't correct wrong word usage. So if you type "from" but you mean "form" the computer will not correct it. Read your letter *out loud* and listen to each word so you don't make a mistake that will be a glaring error to an employer. Before mailing your letter, it's a good idea to have it read by a friend or family member to be sure you didn't miss anything.

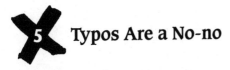 ## Typos Are a No-no

"Nothing's worse than typos," says Stephanie, a human resource manager, who has hired over 500 people. "Once I see a typo—any typo—I know that this is *not* a person we want to hire into our organization." Typos were high on the list of major mistakes that caused employers to reject applicants. Therefore, don't make any.

 ## Do Not Ignore the Stated Criteria

"Applicants who do not address the qualifications or other information requested in the advertisement make a huge mistake. They don't address the employer's needs—at all," said Kelly Bachman, finance manager for a large agricultural company, who found this very frustrating. Many other employers agreed. Applicants simply do not *read* the ad to determine if it's a job they could actually fulfill. Employers want you to take the time to address each specific qualification and state the experience and skills you bring to perform that task or function. That's what's so good about using The Power Impact Technique—you'll easily be able to write a cover letter that matches the employer's advertised criteria, succinctly and effectively. The bottom line is you must show how you are qualified, and if you truly are not, save your time and effort and don't apply.

7 Don't Apply for the Wrong Job

"Job candidates, unqualified for the position advertised, mail in and tell you all about their skills for a totally unrelated position," one manager noted. "We advertised for an executive assistant and got a letter that told all about his marketing skills. Why did he waste his time and mine?" Just mailing in for any job hoping to get noticed for a different position than the one advertised rarely, if ever, works is today's competitive marketplace. This candidate would have gotten much further ahead if he had written a self-marketing letter (see Chapter 6) and mailed it to the head of the marketing department, which was the correct area for the job he wanted.

8 General Letters Are Worthless

Employer after employer after employer told us they hated general cover letters that contained no specific content. "I'm convinced that they can't write, are just lazy, or both," says one HR manager. Specifics sell—specifics and facts in the content of your letter are essential. Accomplishments and evidence of your productivity are the necessary ingredients for a good cover letter. Employers often use your cover letter as a yardstick to measure your writing and communication skills. Therefore, the content must be of substance.

9 Don't Tell the Company That They're Great—They Already Know It

Spending two paragraphs telling a company how great it is doesn't impress anyone. A manager at Nike says: "Forget the superlatives—we know we're a great company. What we don't know (and want to know) is how you can add to our team." In other words, spend your time telling the prospective employer the specifics of how you would excel at the job and the results they might expect—that's what they'll react to.

10 Clueless about My Company

Several managers told us that few people bother to learn anything about the company, and their cover letters reflect that lack of knowledge. A few respondents in our hiring survey offered their thoughts on how you can impress them. "Share some brief knowledge about my company and possibly a success or key effort of ours," suggests Colleen Kill, regional account manager at Searle. "Show interest in the successes of our organization. Explain how you could be part of keeping up the productivity," offers Cathy, a director for a large nonprofit. Many other employers agreed. It seems most want you to "show you know something about my position and needs," as Susan, a senior executive, points out. For many job hunters, details on the company can be challenging to uncover. A quick phone call can often get you a complete job description or a talkative manager who'll provide important insight that will allow you to specifically address the employer's needs. More effort, *yes*—but our employers all felt it made a big difference. In my opinion, it is often the only difference between who gets an interview and who does not. Too many people ignore the need to do a thorough job analysis and company research.

11 The Meat's in the Resumé

Employers want you to offer reasons, skills, and explanations of exactly how you can do the job in the cover letter. This is the first thing they see that tells them all about you as a candidate. If you leave the meat until the resumé, they may never turn the page. State the strongest skills and accomplishments you bring, right up front. You'll get a stronger reaction to your "10 years in project management" when you go on to say you "have always brought projects in on time and on or below budget." A statement that says you've "saved $30,000" will be noticed.

12 No Handwriting, Please

"I absolutely hate it when people send me a handwritten cover letter," says Marie, a human resource manager. "Nothing is more unprofessional than that. I'd like to say we only get them on low-level jobs—but I've seen them from managers and professionals who offer excuses like 'I don't have a printer.' Have they ever heard of Kinko's?" Needless to say, never handwrite under any circumstances unless you *don't* want the position.

13 Avoid Poor Printing Quality

A dot matrix printer too often produces a faint, light type that is difficult to see on the page. If you make it hard to read your letter, you know what will happen—hiring managers won't read it! I recommend you use a friend's laser printer, or go to a copy center to print out a crisp laser copy of your letter and send that. The presentation style of your letter reflects *you*. Be sure you make the grade when your letter is compared to a stack of others that have a sharp and crisp style.

14 They Could Do My Job

The old adage "just get your foot in the door" doesn't seem to apply to most professional positions anymore. It may still work for those in the factory, but not for managers. When an employer is looking at your qualifications and the cover letter says you want an administrative assistant job but the resumé says in your last position you were the department supervisor, the hiring manager gets nervous. No one seeks to hire their own replacement. "It's a mistake when the person is overqualified and doesn't address *why* they would want to change direction for a particular job," Lauren Thomas, a nonprofit managing director, points out. You may have a valid reason to seek a lower-level position, so you may want to note it. Be careful, though, because many employers worry that a desire for a "less stressful position" translates into a burned-out employee who'll not be productive on the job. It's better to write this type of explanation: "I seek to downsize my career to focus on the aspects that I enjoy the most—using the computer, being organized, and supporting my boss's goals and efforts."

15 The Focus Is on You

Many people spend a lengthy amount of time revealing personal information. "It's a mistake to simply tell about oneself," says Laurie Harme, whose position as dean at Macalester College has given her a lot of hiring responsibilities. "I'm impressed, though, when applicants match their skills and experiences to our job description," she adds. Several managers in our survey stated they wanted less "you" information. The Power Impact Technique is designed to achieve the desired goal—it totally focuses your letter on how you can do the employer's job. That's exactly what employers told us they wanted.

 16 Can't Do the Job

I estimated from conversations with many hiring managers and HR personnel that at least 25% of the people who respond to an ad or apply for a posted position do not have the minimal qualifications for the job. Many employers at large companies report that it's as high as 50%. An HR representative at Nintendo told me: "We received over 400 resumés for an accounting manager position, and of course, nearly half were not qualified for the job." Today's job market is too competitive. Years ago, when there was a lack of professionals, you could sweet-talk a manager into trying you out. That's quite challenging to do today. I recommend self-selection: Do not apply if you lack most or all of what's being asked for. Many people apply for jobs where they basically do not fit. I've labeled this the "Want Ad Desperation Syndrome." After spending two hours combing the Sunday paper, you become desperate and apply for jobs where you meet few of the qualifications. Today's want ads in a large city will draw over 200 responses. That's a lot of competition and, in many cases, a lot of wasted effort if your skills aren't a good fit for the job described. I've always suggested *not* writing letters until Monday— it's amazing how 24 hours can help you eliminate half the ads you thought were okay the morning before. It's not quantity, but quality and *quantifying your abilities* to meet the employer's needs that will get you noticed. Concentrate your efforts on locating jobs that match your skills. You'll find much more success in that approach.

17 No One's Home

When you are job hunting, it's imperative that you have either a person or device answering your phone to get those important calls from employers. Hard to believe in today's world of voice mail and answering machines that some people still don't have one. I was assisting an employer with screening applicants, and one of them had no answering machine. I tried twice, and then forgot about that person as I arranged interviews for some of the others on the list. You could be forgotten, too—make sure this doesn't happen.

18 Children Should Not Take Your Messages

Nothing is more frustrating than calling an applicant whose child answers the phone and is not able to clearly take down the message concerning the interview. One HR manager offered, "Job hunters miss opportunities when I call and a young child appears unable to write down the message and take my phone number correctly. I immediately question the applicant's judgment and their potential effectiveness on the job every time this occurs." Isn't it funny how simple things can be such a negative influence? More than once, employers have been put off by a rude teenager. I recommend that you carefully instruct family members, or simply install a separate line with an answering machine to obtain potential employers' calls. Mistakes like a phone number written incorrectly can cost you a job.

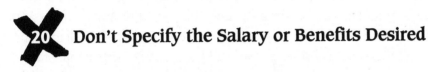

19 Phone Etiquette Doesn't Exist

Keep the message on your answering machine simple and professional. Funny, weird, or risqué messages might be cool for your friends, but they will not impress employers while you're job hunting.

20 Don't Specify the Salary or Benefits Desired

I recommend you never offer this information in your letter on your own initiative unless you really want the employer to disregard you. A significant number of the hiring managers we surveyed were downright offended, angered, and hostile about job hunters who write, "I need $36,000 plus medical, dental, and retirement benefits" when no salary information was even requested. It has such a negative impact—it focuses totally on you and your needs—and not the employer's. Don't do it.

21 Do Not Apply if the Stated Salary Is Too Low

Employers state a salary range to attract people who are willing to work at *that* compensation level. I recommend you apply accordingly. Many employers are frustrated by applicants who totally disregard the stated salary knowing they need or want much more than is being offered. "Salaries are stated to allow individuals the option to *not* apply if it's too low," states an HR manager at a Fortune 500 company. Tracy White, a director at the Washington Society of CPAs, adds: "We state a salary with words 'firm' after it in our ad and we still get dozens of letters that state they want something higher." Assuming an employer will find thousands more than what was budgeted rarely happens. They state the salary and expect, if you apply, that means you are desiring to work for that stated level of compensation.

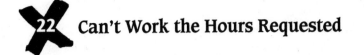

22 Can't Work the Hours Requested

One hiring criterion paramount in employers' minds is, "Will you be able and willing to work all the hours we need?" As more Americans seek flextime at work to accommodate family needs, commuter traffic, and academic or leisure pursuits, amount of work hours has become an increasingly larger employer problem to solve. Your personal obligations can be a major conflict with the employer's stated hours. Full-time positions usually mandate 40 hours per week, and you can't always expect to run out the door at 5:01 P.M. Don't apply for jobs that have hours you can't or don't want to keep. Likewise, be sure to address your willingness to work evenings and weekends for their position, if it is required, and that you would be able to cover those hours. Elizabeth, owner of a service company, offered this insight on her hiring needs: "We have a lot of part-time jobs. They are just that, *part-time*. I get angered by applicants who apply and the first thing that they bring up in the interview is: 'When will this turn to full-time?' They aren't honest with themselves or us when they mail in their resumés. It's a huge waste of both our time."

23 Avoid Sending Salary History

I asked several questions concerning salary and found that 23% of employers surveyed requested salary history in their recruitment process. Why? To screen out those who were too high or too low and to determine the average amount that people are paid. Questions on salary are an employer's trick to *screen you out* of the competition. I have included some cover letters on exactly how to answer these questions in Chapter 4, but suffice it to say—unless it is *required,* I recommend that you never send your salary history. If you are compelled to respond, offer a range that gives you more latitude to not be screened out, plus some leeway to negotiate salary if and when you are later offered the job.

24 No Address or Phone Number Is Included

Always create a letterhead at the top of your page that contains this vital information. One HR rep sent along a cover letter that had no address or phone number on it. She sarcastically wrote, "Don't you just love this? We couldn't contact this person even if we wanted to." I recommend you include your address and always include your home telephone number. It is not advisable to list your work number. That way, when an employer calls you'll be able to ask questions about the job and get directions without worrying that someone at work is listening.

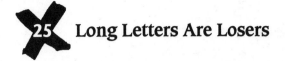

25 Long Letters Are Losers

By using The Power Impact Technique, you'll indeed be succinct, high-lighting only the major points—just enough to get the employer's attention. Many managers told us they do not want (and in several cases do not *read*) long letters. Karma Reairs, HR manager at Dean Foods, says: "Stick to the point. Just hit the highlights that would separate the applicant from the crowd without rehashing the entire resumé." Heather, another personnel director, added: "The worst mistake job hunters make is writing letters that are just too long." Employers preferred concise but detailed and specific letters. *One page was the overall preference.* Rarely should it take two. I recommend you stick to one page.

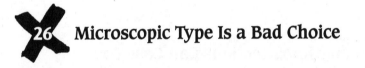

26 Microscopic Type Is a Bad Choice

Letters must be easy to read. Every manager communicated this to us. This means no font size that requires a magnifying glass to read it. Keep the font—such as Palatino, Helvetica, or styles similar to these—at point size 12 or 13. Too many job hunters will reduce the font size to get the entire letter onto one page. Carefully editing is a better alternative.

27 Thinking Presentation Doesn't Matter

Think so? "Overall appearance is the one thing that is the most important, followed by it being an intelligently written letter," Oris Barber, director of human resources, noted. Our survey respondents emphatically wanted a letter that is professionally formatted, concise, and easy to read. Sandy, an HR recruiter, said: "The cover letter is my first impression of the person. Professionalism, a good format, and the letter style influences me to *read more or not read the letter at all.*" Make sure you pay extra attention to the layout and professionalism. Indeed, the visual appeal of the letter makes an important difference and is influential.

28 Grammar Imperfections Can Cost You

Employers said blatant grammatical mistakes were a major turnoff. So be careful, and ask a friend to read your letter to confirm that your points are well written and clear. Several human resource directors and hiring managers stated they used the cover letter as an active representation of a person's written communication skills. With that yardstick in mind, you can realize exactly how important writing a good cover letter truly is.

29 Unsubstantiated Bragging Backfires

"Don't oversell," says Karen Martin, national sales manager, who's seen a lot of unsubstantiated boasting from job applicants. "I see a lot of puffed-up statements. Usually this is because their qualifications are thin." Don't create exaggerations no one will believe. Grandiose statements like "terrific closer," "one of the top salesmen you'll ever hire," "I'm the best," "I can sell anything" are all unproven claims without the substance of specified achievements to back up the statement. But when you use the "Actions equals Results" concept that's part of The Power Impact Technique taught in this book, you'll learn how to state the truth in the correct way to get attention. You will back up all statements with facts—not just rhetoric.

30 Just Wanting to Be in Management Is Not Enough

"I've seen endless numbers who say they want to be in 'management,' yet they show no evidence that they have earned that right," says Jim, a top executive at a Fortune 500 company. "We must see, by both experience and, more important, behavior, that applicants have shown leadership and contributed to the success of the team. How you get along with others is a critical element most never address." Reassess your background. Look at volunteer work, company committees, and projects you've been involved with to offer evidence to pique these employers' interest. Demonstrating team leadership to get the job done, innovation, coaching fellow employees, and a commitment to empowering others are essentials Jim suggested you point out in your letter as you seek a higher level of responsibility.

31 Not Showing a True Interest

Hiring is changing, and I saw a lot of evidence that both corporate and nonprofits alike wanted to hear about why the job was a good fit and of real interest to the applicant. Brian Kirby Unti, head of a nonprofit, offered these insights reflective of our changing times: "I've changed the way I go about hiring people in the last three years. I used to rely heavily upon trying to find an applicant who met the requirements of the job description—previous history and specific skills. Now I identify people who have a real passion to work in our industry and who can imagine possibilities for how the job might unfold. What scores points with me now is resourcefulness, creativity and imagination, flexibility, being a team player, ability to cope with change, and willingness to try new things." When you offer to bring your professional desire, passion, talents, and previous accomplishments to a new job, you've got a winning combination.

32 Don't Botch Their Names

A Fortune 500 HR manager took great offense at having her name misspelled. Frequently, she noted, letters are addressed to the manager (in this case, Mr. Kim Rice) when the receiver is actually a woman. She went on to say that it was impressive to her when people had taken the time to find out her name and send the letter addressed specifically to her, instead of the generic "Dear Personnel Manager." Anna, another HR manager, said: "The worst cover letter mistake I've ever seen had the cover letter addressed to me, spelled my name wrong, and the letter begins, 'Dear ____ ,' with someone else's name in it!"

33 Poor Salutations Start You Off on the Wrong Foot

A question I'm often asked in my seminars is: "Whom do I address the cover letter to when there's no name?" Well, "Dear Sir/Dear Madam" is old-fashioned and "To whom it may concern" is outdated. My first recommendation is to try to obtain the person's name by calling the organization and asking for it. If you aren't able to get it, then address your letter to: "Dear Company," "Dear Title" (e.g., Dear Marketing Director), or "Dear Manager"—all are acceptable alternatives.

34 Sloppiness

We receive numerous complaints about sloppiness in format, structure, and even poor penmanship. Professionalism must be paramount in your mind—no cross-outs, ink scratches (besides your nicely written signature), or crumpled or marked-up paper. Many noticed the envelope to see if it was typed, laser-printed, or written, commenting that sloppy penmanship was a serious error and reflected poorly on the candidate. One VP wrote: "I always look at the signature and envelope. I like a professional look—the kind that demonstrates the person operates with high standards. Nothing's worse than envelopes that are almost illegible. They make me wonder about the person's performance on the job and communication in writing to staff and other managers—I worry that they'll be misunderstood, causing us all problems." It's clearly evident to me that employers need to see the very best you have to offer, even on the smallest details. Typed or laser-printed envelopes make the best impression.

35 Don't Expect the Employer to Find a Need for You to Fill

Many job hunters make this mistake. It's almost the norm for career changers and new college graduates. They simply generalize all their experience in hopes that the employer will take the time to decipher the skills and figure out where the person could fit in. That's your responsibility. It is virtually impossible to tell an employer specifically how you'll do a job well when you have no particular job in mind. My best advice is to take some time and do some career exploration. Take a class or visit a qualified career counselor to aid you in your self-assessment. Identify two or three jobs you feel you could excel in. Pursue those. If you do not, you may be continually frustrated by your lack of response from (and success with) employers.

36 Using Buzzwords Can Backfire

Adrian, a human resource manager, pointed out a significant error when she told us that she can quickly recognize an unqualified candidate by the use of obvious buzzwords without the facts to back up the lingo. Although it's important to use industry language (e.g., TQM), I recommend you use it only where and when it illustrates an important contribution you have made. And never use a buzzword if you are not sure what it means. In this case, TQM stands for Total Quality Management, a common manufacturing term.

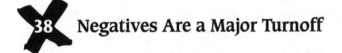 37 Desperation by Any Other Name Is Still Desperation

One HR manager for a Fortune 500 company told us about a dreadful story in which the applicant's house had been burned down and he *really* needed a job. Any job. When I asked what the HR manager did, she said: "Did? Well, nothing. I felt very sorry for the person, but we hire people who have skills to offer." Desperation on your part won't convince an employer to give you the job. That rarely works anymore, even for entry-level factory or labor jobs. It's the wrong approach to use to get hired, even if it is true. Employers want you to focus on what you can do for them instead of, as in this case, what an employer could obviously do for this applicant.

38 Negatives Are a Major Turnoff

Rose, a human resource manager, told me: "Job hunters fail to see the impact they create when they offer negative information. The cover letter (or interview) is not the place to lambaste an old employer. If they only realized just how much this action *negatively reflects on the applicant,* they would never do it." When you use The Power Impact Technique, you will always keep your letters positive. You will stress your skills and accomplishments, and nothing negative is ever mentioned.

39 Don't Include the Employer's Want Ad

Gene, the head of HR for a Fortune 100 company, told me about a new thing job hunters have begun to do that is a "complete waste of time"— mailing in a copy of the actual want ad with your cover letter and resumé. "I don't need it and I don't want it," he told me. As long as you reference the job title that you want to be considered for in your letter, that's enough.

40 Leaving Out Important Credentials

Special designations such as MBA, J.D., Ph.D., or PE are a vital ingredient in your package of skills. Major titles such as these need to be placed in the letterhead, after your name, at the very top of your letter. Instead of writing "Mary Stephens," it's more powerful and impressive to employers to have your top line read "Mary Stephens, MBA."

 **41 No Signature**

"We often get letters that are unsigned," noted Josh, a personnel recruiter for a prominent retail store chain. A few other human resource managers also pointed this out. A good, clear signature is a must on every letter you mail.

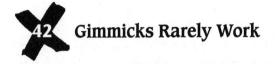

Gimmicks Rarely Work

"People will do anything for attention—most of it never works," said one news director at a prominent TV station. "Every day someone tries a new trick—flowers, candy, even a box of cookies wrapped in their resumé. I might have eaten the cookies, but it didn't get them the job." We had numerous comments from our hiring managers that gimmicks, designer papers, oversized envelopes, and using Federal Express or other overnight services do not improve your chances of getting an interview. They often prove to be a negative. "The clever gimmicks are usually to hide a lack of true substance," a senior vice president wrote. "Wild-colored papers and designs are the worst mistakes people make," said Susan, a store manager. "Tell people *no* picture on their cover letter," advises Tom Wermerkichen, human resource manager for Mustang Manufacturing. Nothing will replace a simple letter with solid facts focused on how you can excel at performing the job. It's the meat of proven experience, skills, and accomplishments that truly gets attention and keeps the employer's interest long enough to call you in for an interview.

Summary

The bottom line that came out of our survey was best summarized by Melanie Prinsen, a VP of human resources: "Applicants *must use a cover letter.* Indicate the job you are applying for, make it one page, state your interest in the position, and include a paragraph or two that describes your work experience, special projects, or qualifications in a way that tells us how well you'll perform on the job."

Focus on how you'll meet the employer's needs. That is the key! That's what employers say they want. That is exactly what you'll give them when you use The Power Impact Technique to write your cover letters. Remember, *96%* of all hiring managers surveyed selected The Power Impact Technique as their preferred cover letter style. The conclusion is that a strong, well-written letter *will* get the employer's attention.

THE POWER IMPACT TECHNIQUE

3

"I can't believe there's no cover letter" says human resource director Deanna. "Seems to me if they are too lazy to write a good one, they'll be a slacker on the job, too. Candidates need to realize that their letter is the first thing I see when I sort through my stack of resumés. Unless there are some good specifics, I will often not bother to go to the resumé. I know that almost all people write their own cover letters and that the letter is a true sampling of their writing and communication skill, whereas resumés can be bought and 'doctored' by others, so they are less representative."

Hiring managers agree—good cover letters are very influential. Since the average professional position usually competes against 200 applicants or more, you absolutely *must* grab the employer's attention in your opening sentence. We've discussed in our last chapter how the two typical openings fail miserably. The worst culprit is, "I am writing to apply for the ad that I saw in Sunday's paper." This opening is used by most applicants, so when employers are reviewing dozens of candidates, they've seen these words so often their mind automatically jumps into a scan mode. Likewise, the second opening—"You're a great company"—tells the employer something they already know.

Neither opening captures the employer's attention. The Power Impact Technique begins with a strong opening that focuses on filling the employer's needs. My clients who have used this technique for years have had positive feedback from employers and gotten interviews! Almost

CAREER COACH
fact

Our employer survey results easily confirmed that they expect and want to see a well-written, articulate cover letter.

every hiring manager surveyed selected The Power Impact Technique as the preferred letter-writing style. Once you've learned this writing style, you'll never spend hours slaving over a cover letter again.

> **The Power Impact Technique is basically a two-step process:**
>
> 1. Analyze the job—both the noted and assumed needs—and determine the most important skills the employer is looking for.
> 2. Immediately address how you will meet the employer's needs.

"A poor opening paragraph is why many job hunters fail," said CEO Robert Waldt. "It is usually a common, general sentence. You need to immediately establish something unique about the candidate. I like to see the particular reason—background or experience—that tells me why I should hire the person up front at the start of the letter."

Over two-thirds of our hiring managers agreed with Robert and noted that a common mistake made in writing cover letters was a poor opening paragraph.

The Power Impact Technique begins your letter with a strong opening sentence that emphasizes the major selling points and skills you would bring to the job. It offers actions and results—the winning formula that really has employers taking notice. Look at the difference between the typical opening, "I'm applying for the ad in Sunday's paper," and a couple of openings using The Power Impact Technique:

✔ Ten years in senior management with proven expertise in international purchasing for a Fortune 100 company . . .

✔ A proven track record in corporate fundraising . . .

✔ A solid background developing new business and increasing sales . . .

✔ Strong retail store management experience with proven expertise to improve sales and customer service and motivate employees . . .

As you can see, these openers are eye-catching, designed to get employers to really read what you can do. The secret lies in simply addressing employers' needs right up front. After all, these are the necessary skills and experience they are seeking.

CAREER COACH *fact*

Cover letters require a compelling opening sentence.

The body of your letter is used to demonstrate "proof" that you can perform the duties desired. To develop this proof, make an outline of the important points that the employer wants. Just underline the major items from the want ad or job-opening announcement if you have one. Whenever possible, use your network to gather any inside information on what's most important to that employer for that job. Always keep in mind this one thing: What is it that they need me to do in this job to do it well? Then consider what have you done in your previous jobs. That's the experience we want to emphasize. For example, the employer might want computer skills or teamwork, both important points in many jobs today.

The next step is to ask yourself—What were the *results* of my efforts on previous jobs, projects, or tasks that I've undertaken? There's the key—to compose your letter, just highlight the duties and skills needed by referencing your abilities to perform them and offering any known results from your past efforts as the proof that you *can* do the job.

Hiring managers in our survey want concise letters. Keep the body of the letter short, not more than one page. Also, be sure to continually demonstrate how you'll be able to do the job. Many of these points are simply shortened versions of content from your resumé. Conclude your letter with this power phrase: "*The valuable contributions I'd bring to your organization . . .*" This shows you're a team player who's productive and focused on being an asset to the employer. Never forget what is constantly running through the employer's mind: "*What's in it for me if I hire this person? Can they do the job? Will they fit in?*"

Your cover letter must develop enough interest to get the employer to want to turn the page, look at your resumé, and say, "*Let's call this one in for an interview.*"

Success Stories

Now let's examine The Power Impact Technique letters. We'll look at six clients, examining their want ads and Power Impact Technique letters.* I've also included their resumés to give you a complete picture of the whole package and writing process.† These are real people facing actual situations you may encounter. They are perfect illustrations of how effective The Power Impact Technique truly is.

MARY—

Her challenge was to leave her own business and go back to work for an employer. She worried that not having a college degree would be an obstacle.

Mary's friend had told her that Airborne had a job opening for a trainer. Mary owned a training business but was tired of the long hours spent soliciting business and not actually training. The idea of no longer being the business owner appealed to her.

   She contacted me to help her apply for the job. She had no resumé. She'd spent over 20 years with a large company and then went into business for herself. Mary lacked confidence in her skills and wasn't sure they'd appeal to any employer. She was also concerned because she lacked a college degree. She thought this whole process was unlikely to lead to anything, but she wanted to try. In actuality, it's pretty common to devalue what you have done. Women are notorious for not giving themselves credit for their accomplishments. Forget what your mother taught you about being humble. It is important to boast if you want a job. You have to carve out clearly for the employer a vivid description of your past performance and talents if you want to get hired in today's market.

   In Mary's case, I pointed out to her that she was a talented woman who'd proven year after year that she was a good trainer. Since she had no long-term goals to go into administration, I was not concerned about her lack of a college degree. I felt that her experience, especially since she

* All clients' names have been changed to ensure confidentiality. Similar companies and colleges have also been selected. All other details specific to each client are true and accurate as depicted in each cover letter and resumé in this book exactly as the employers saw them.
   † The resumés in this chapter were all written using The Goldmining Technique™ illustrated in Robin Ryan's book, *Winning Resumés* (Wiley).

had spent 10 years in training with a large phone company, would weigh heavily in her favor.

So, how did she do?

Competition was keen for this corporate trainer position. Mary's cover letter and resumé beat out 405 others. After three interviews, Airborne was convinced she was the right one. Mary landed her dream job after writing *only one cover letter!* Now that may not happen all the time, but it does happen for some of my career counseling clients. Let's examine how Mary and I created this cover letter. I've even included Mary's resumé so you'll be able to see how we took some information directly from it and created the bulleted points used in Mary's letter. Also notice that both the resumé and cover letter are specific in addressing the skills the employer required to succeed in this job.

Mary landed her dream job after writing only one cover letter!

Mary Talker

1530 Lake Avenue, Apt. 12D
Seattle, WA 98102
(206) 555-0111

CAREER OBJECTIVE: **Trainer**

SUMMARY OF QUALIFICATIONS

Nineteen years in corporate training and management in a major US company with 15,000 employees. Proven expertise in platform skills, learning styles, curriculum development and improvement of employee job performance.

PROFESSIONAL EXPERIENCE

Training

- Fifteen years in training and curriculum development for Management and Staff in a $10 billion dollar company employing over 15,000.
- Taught thousands of classes, workshops and programs in three-hour sessions up to multiple-week format to adult learners. Adapted material to learning style of each group for maximum retention.
- Instructed Employees in job and management building skills including Supervision, Team Building, Communication Styles, Train-The-Trainer, Sales, Mentor/ Coaching, Job Performance and Customer Service.
- Created and utilized training evaluations to maintain a high level of instruction and retention.

Curriculum Development

- Created 15 new training programs for managers and non-management employees. Topics were designed for performance enhancement and skill building.
- Designed numerous training materials including handouts, charts, graphs, job aids, overheads and audio cassettes.
- Developed Office Procedures manual for departmental and operational use by managers and non-management personnel.

Management

- Twenty years in customer service management for a $10 billion dollar telecommunications company, supervising Commercial Account Representatives.

WORK HISTORY

Trainer, Seminars, Inc., Seattle, WA, 1990-Present
Trainer/Customer Service, MCI Communications, Seattle, WA, 1964-1990

Let's analyze the want ad:

TRAINER

National freight company seeks professional with
5 years training experience to teach leadership
and management training.

After examining her resumé and the employer's ad, we used The Power Impact Technique to write the first sentence. We decided it needed to summarize her years in training as we felt this was the most important part to the employer. We opened with:

Fifteen years in corporate training and management for a major U.S. employer.

The big eye-catchers here were the *15 years in corporate training* and the fact that it was also *for a large employer.*

Then we continued with the job analysis. Always determine the skills the employer wants, both the NOTED and ASSUMED needs. Really think about what specific skills or experience the person must have to perform the job. We felt, for Mary, these were "demonstrated speaking skills," and "good participant evaluation ratings." They are the action and the important result of her training effectiveness. Others were "created curriculum," "experience teaching management and staff," and "adult learners," which is exactly the employer's population that must be trained. We highlighted these (excerpted mostly from her resumé) and developed the key points for her letter.

Here are the impact statements that we wrote:

✔ Taught thousands of classes and workshops to managers and staff on management and leadership topics.

✔ Created and adapted curriculum to meet the learning needs of various groups of adult learners.

✔ Consistently received high evaluations from participants.

✔ Created 15 new training programs to meet the needs of 15,000 managers and staff for a major company.

We always end our letter with a "valuable contributions" statement. It's also a good idea to give your phone number, even though you've listed it at the top of the page.

I would like to discuss in greater detail the valuable contributions I would make to Airborne. I can be reached at (206) 555-0111.

This ending reinforces that you are focused on meeting the employer's needs and becoming a valued asset to them. It's clear, strong, and quite effective!

Here was Mary's Power Impact Technique cover letter:

Mary Talker
1530 Lake Avenue, Apt. 12D
Seattle, Washington 98102
(206) 555-0111

Mary beat out 405 others to land this job!

January 18, 1996

Dear Airborne,

Fifteen years in corporate training and management for a major U.S. employer is the background I'd bring to your trainer position.

Highlights of my background include:

- Taught thousands of classes and workshops to managers and staff on management and leadership topics.
- Created and adapted curriculum to meet the learning needs of various groups of adult learners.
- Consistently received high evaluations from participants.
- Created 15 new training programs to meet the needs of 15,000 managers and staff for a major company.

I would like to discuss in greater detail the valuable contributions I would make to Airborne. I can be reached at (206) 555-0111.

Your time and consideration is most appreciated.

Sincerely,

Mary Talker

Mary Talker

You can see how impressive and specific this letter is. The proof of its effectiveness lies in the fact that she applied to only one employer and got hired.

DIANE—

Her challenge was to change from one career to an entirely new one.

Diane had been in the food industry's research area seven years ago. Her last job was as a computer aided designer—a highly technical position that paid well, but Diane found little joy in the work. During our coaching sessions she targeted a position she truly wanted—sales representative for a food company. Diane worked hard at the career-changing process. She improved her interview skills, networked, and joined a related association; the challenge to move into the new field where she had no true sales experience was an obstacle—but not impossible. There were several positions where she came in second, but the employers chose someone who had a proven sales record. Many times, all it takes is to keep trying and learn more about the field to effectively sell the skills you do have.

Here is the want ad Diane responded to:

GOURMET COFFEE SALES
EXPRESS UNLIMITED

A traditional Italian roaster is seeking territory sales-person to join our family. Minimum 2 years successful sales experience, team player, exceptional attitude and strong organizational skills to qualify.

We developed Diane's resumé and cover letter to emphasize her background in customer service, sales support, and presentations.

Diane Sales

7 Water Crest Way
Houston, TX 11111
(713) 555-0111

CAREER OBJECTIVE: **Sales Representative**

SUMMARY OF QUALIFICATIONS

Eight years in technical sales support and new product development within the food industry. Extensive product knowledge with strong presentation and demonstration skills. Focused on customer service, exceeding goals and finding new marketing and business opportunities.

PROFESSIONAL EXPERIENCE

Customer Service/Sales

- Technical sales support on a new innovative food/produce product including: demonstrations, customer problem resolutions, and quality assurance for customers. Sales exceeded all company goals by second year.
- Presented formal presentations and demonstrations to food growers/customers as part of extensive marketing and educational campaign on new, higher quality product, justifying significantly higher product price. Overcame extensive customer resistance.
- Developed new quality control procedures to enhance the productivity and customer satisfaction on new food products.
- Responsible for persuading top management to re-direct marketing efforts by establishing significant new sales benefits on the new product. Increased product market supply by 20% yielding significant market share advances.

Product Development

- Managed research development on new food/produce product including: field studies, testing, budget, and documentation through its initial market introduction.
- Wrote comprehensive trial study research report for top management based on new product research data. 87-page report included: field studies, location data, methods/materials, conclusions, and both product and market recommendations.
- Developed and implemented new growing procedures that increased quality and production by 10%.

WORK HISTORY

Computer Aided Designer, Engineering Corporation of America,
Houston, TX, 1989-1995
Manager of Technical Services, Genetics, Inc., Dallas, TX 1984-1987
Manager, J&M Agricultural Co., Dallas, TX 1982-1984
Assistant Production Manager, Transplant Co., Dallas, TX 1981-1982

VOLUNTEER ACTIVITIES/ASSOCIATIONS

Master Gardener, University of Texas, Cooperative Extension, 1995
Landscape Committee Chair, Remington Homeowners Association, 1995
Women's Food Industry Network, 1995

EDUCATION

Master of Science in Agriculture, Cal Poly, San Luis Obispo, CA, 1980
Bachelor of Arts in Psychology, San Jose State University, San Jose, CA, 1974

Looking at her resumé, you'll notice we made the most of what Diane had done. Our emphasis was to play up her old skills and downplay her recent job over the last seven years. Upon examining the ad, we opened with the following:

Eight years in technical sales support within the food industry.

This immediately drew in the employer. Next we analyzed exactly what a sales rep needs to do on the job. The formal presentations and food demonstrations are marketing activities that were relevant. Finally, we wanted to point out strong organizational skills and customer assistance.

The sales manager for the coffee company responded when he got this letter:

Diane Sales
7 Water Crest Way
Houston, TX 11111
(713) 555-0111

November 5, 1996

Sales Manager
Express Unlimited
7 Myrtle Street
Houston, TX 55555

Dear Sales Manager,

Eight years in technical sales support within the food industry with proven marketing and product development skills is the background I'd bring to Express Unlimited as your Sales Representative.

Highlights of my experience include:

- Sales support on a new innovative food/produce product with sales exceeding company goals by the second year.
- Formal presentations and demonstrations to food growers as part of an extensive marketing and educational team campaign on new, high quality product, justifying significantly higher product price. Overcame extensive customer resistance.
- Development of new quality control procedures to enhance customer satisfaction with new food products.
- Good organizational and communication skills, the ability to take initiative and to give customers the pro-active and responsive service that builds long term customer relationships.

I feel there is a great deal that I can bring to Express Unlimited and its customers. Please contact me at (713) 555-0111 to arrange a meeting to discuss the valuable contributions I could make as part of your team.

Sincerely,

Diane Sales

Diane Sales

Diane landed the job and has been very happy with the new position.

Diane has done very well in her new field in sales. Enthusiasm and the desire to excel aided Diane in making this move. It required a lot of tenacious effort. Career changing is never an easy process, but in Diane's case she reports that it sure was worth all the effort.

JOAN—

Her challenge was to find a new position after being fired.

Of all the challenges facing us in our careers, being fired is the hardest and certainly the most stressful to endure. You begin to doubt yourself, your abilities, and whether you'll get a new position. It's a painful experience that most workers will go through at some point during their working career.

I began to work with Joan when she was fired as the director of a nonprofit organization. The board criticized Joan's abilities, sighting poor budget skills. She admitted she wasn't too good at office politics, and that also hurt her in this position. It became apparent to me that Joan had a lot of strong skills that simply needed to be aligned with the right organization. She lacked self-confidence because her last few months on the job had been demoralizing.

As her job search progressed, Joan proved to be a "networking queen." Over the years, she had helped many people with their job hunting activities. Now, she found everyone was eager to help her.

It took several months before she learned about this position:

EXECUTIVE DIRECTOR—THE GARDENS FOUNDATION

A 3,000 member support organization for The National Park Arboretum, is seeking a full-time Executive Director. Responsibilities include: raising funds, administering the Foundation's office, coordinating volunteers, increasing membership, and advocating a new master plan for the Arboretum.

Qualifications: Management experience; proven abilities working with donors, volunteers, local governments, academic institutions and the public. Experience in fundraising, outreach, and public relations is essential. BA, BS or MBA degree. Interest in and some knowledge of ornamental horticulture is desirable.

We worked on her resumé and emphasized her strengths: managing people, special events, public relations, and media.

Joan Director
6800 175th Avenue NE
San Francisco, CA 33333
(415) 555-0111

CAREER OBJECTIVE: **Non-Profit Executive Director**

SUMMARY OF QUALIFICATIONS

Thirteen years of progressive nonprofit experience with last three as Executive Director with strong proven fundraising, media relations, event planning, and leadership abilities.

PROFESSIONAL EXPERIENCE

Management

- Daily operations of not-for-profit organization with staff of six, 30 member board of governors, and 100+ volunteers.
- Well-developed office systems that allow for detailed tracking of events, and excellent organization and handling of multiple demanding tasks at once.
- Personnel functions include: recruiting, screening, hiring, terminations, performance evaluations, improved employee handbook, negotiate compensation packages, and training.
- Converted office's manual system to computerized system. Doubled charity's annual giving.

Special Events/Fundraising

- 175+ special events organized including: fundraisers, galas, auctions, luncheons, dinners, political debates, lectures, seminars, continuing education, conferences and conventions.
- Recruited top name local and national speakers waiving fees up to thousands of dollars.
- Contract negotiations: meeting space, lodging, meals, vendors, advertising and printing needs.
- Volunteer management: recruiting, selecting, training, managing hundreds of volunteers.

Communications

- Produced brochures, ad copy, public service announcements, news releases, press releases, annual reports, newsletters, company publications, business reports and correspondence.
- Accomplished public speaker with groups from 1 to 2500.
- Publication reporter for column.
- Instructor, Santa Clara Extension, "Special Event Fundraising."
- Grant writing with 90% funding success.

Media Relations

- KOOW 3-minute commentary: wrote, aired, unedited.
- Press liaison to KGO, KRON, and KPIX TV, numerous radio, statewide newspapers with solid contacts in all media areas with emphasis on positive exposure.
- Effectively handled controversial media "hot potato."

WORK HISTORY

Executive Director, Business Center Club, San Francisco, CA, 1990-1993
Development Director, American Lung Association, San Francisco, CA, 1988-1990
Special Events Representative, Research Center, Berkeley, CA, 1986-1988
Special Events Manager, Children's Hospital, Oakland, CA, 1980-1986

EDUCATION

Bachelor of Arts, Communications, Santa Clara University, CA, 1980, *cum laude*

We needed to stress Joan's management experience and identify her strengths, so we opened her cover letter with the following:

With thirteen years of progressive nonprofit management in the Bay region, I bring strong administrative skills to your position of Executive Director of The Gardens Foundation. My strengths are in the areas of administration, communication, special events, and media relations.

This quickly brought to light that Joan had the skills to do the job. Resumés from 265 other applicants, many with previous experience, were vying for the opportunity. We illustrated the size of her last organization and staff plus mentioned success in obtaining grants from some prominent local companies. Mentioning her budget experience was also included.

Here's Joan's cover letter:

Joan Director
6800 175th Avenue NE
San Francisco, CA 33333
(415) 555-0111

June 4, 1995

Executive Director of Search Committee
The Gardens Foundation
1515 51st Street
San Francisco, CA 94104

Dear Executive Director of Search Committee,

With thirteen years of progressive nonprofit management in the Bay region, I bring strong administrative skills to your position of Executive Director of The Gardens Foundation. My strengths are in the areas of administration, communication, special events, and media relations.

For the past three years, I have managed a 501(c)(3) organization with a $250,000 budget and board comprised of 30 members, with a staff of 6. This has given me a broad base of experience in budget preparation and fiscal and personnel management. Additionally, I have been successful in writing grant proposals and administering grants from local companies such TCI and Macy's. In terms of curriculum development, I have overseen over 40 programs annually which inform members of civic issues pertaining to the Bay region.

My resumé is enclosed for your review. It would be my pleasure to discuss the position of Executive Director with you. To arrange a meeting, I can be reached at (415) 555-0111.

Thank you for your time and consideration.

Sincerely,

Joan Director

Joan Director

After two interviews, Joan landed this terrific new job.

Joan found the entire job search process a difficult learning experience. Her esteem and confidence had really been hurt by being terminated. She is very happy with her new organization and was quite grateful when the whole process was finally over.

RICH—

His challenge was to find a new job after being fired from the only company he had worked at for 17 years.

Rich's situation is like many others who are in senior management. He spent his whole career at one company, moving up the ranks at one of the country's top insurance companies into a senior executive position.

A reengineering program was set in place two years before within Rich's company, and a subordinate soon became his boss. He was demoted. Although upset by this demotion, he felt that the price was too high to compete to keep his old job. The new boss was a hard-driven workaholic who spent 70 hours a week at the job. Rich had a family and chose to spend more time with them and less on the job. As sometimes happens, long-term employees can appear to coast at their jobs and are not always viewed as vital producers or team players when new managers take over. In the end, that led to his being fired.

Rich was angry and resentful when I first met him. After a session or two, he quickly recovered and was putting positive efforts into his job search. Other executives warned Rich that most senior executives at the CFO level had a difficult time finding another position. It averaged six to nine months—longer for several who had tight one-industry experience like he did. It just goes to show you, others *can* be wrong. Within one month, Rich had heard of an opening from a colleague.

Here's the job announcement that Rich and I worked on:

CHIEF FINANCIAL OFFICER—VACANCY

Massachusetts' largest non-profit association seeks a Chief Financial Officer to guide us. The candidate must possess no less than ten years experience in accounting and finance. Qualified candidates should mail resumés to:

Search Committee
Massachusetts Education Association
Kennedy Plaza, Suite 1800
Boston, MA 02155
Attn: Manager of Personnel
Competitive salary and excellent benefits program are offered.

Richard M. Cash, CPA

1700 Commonwealth Avenue
Boston, MA 02111
(617) 555-0111

CAREER OBJECTIVE: Chief Financial Officer

SUMMARY OF QUALIFICATIONS

Fifteen years in senior financial management with proven expertise in administration of financial policies, accounting, budgeting, financial analysis, banking and computer systems. Excel at team development and building positive relationships with other departments and outside parties.

PROFESSIONAL EXPERIENCE

Assistant Vice President/Controller, Prudential, Boston, MA, 1979-1996
(Promoted from Assistant Controller, promoted from Accounting Manager)
Senior Accountant, Deloitte & Touche, Boston, MA, 1974-1979

Finance

- Managed the financial operation of a real estate subsidiary with $500 million in assets and $75 million of annual revenue. Complete leadership over accounting, payroll, banking, cash management, risk management, records, computer systems and administrative services.
- Developed and implemented accounting policies and procedures, performed financial analysis and supervised financial reporting for a subsidiary with $3.8 billion of investments.
- Reorganized three departments, eliminating four positions with annual savings of $200,000 while improving productivity and internal accounting controls through increased automation and cross-training.
- Developed annual and five year budgets, and performed strategic planning and forecasting.

Administration

- Managed the human resource functions for seven departments consisting of 35 employees including job descriptions, performance evaluations, hiring, terminations, compensation, conflict resolution and employee training.
- Complete leadership over central records, purchasing, mail distribution, telephone system, office equipment and service contracts.
- Developed new auditing system over third party agencies dealing with revenue collection and claims processing.
- Developed comprehensive policies, procedures and training manuals that increased efficiency and internal accounting control.

Computer Systems

- Coordinated periodic systems upgrades and ongoing conversions from manual processing, including: needs analysis, research, hardware/software selection and acquisition and staff training. The automation resulted in increased productivity, accuracy and data accessibility for strategic planning and decision-making.
- Developed customized software applications for improved budgeting, investment analysis and revenue recognition.

EDUCATION

Bachelor of Arts, Accounting, Bentley College, MA, 1974

Rich had a strong financial background that would be easily recognized. He'd supervised a large department and had investing, plus cash management, experience. But that would only be part of the equation. He needed to show interest in the organization and personalize his desire to join the team. Here's what he wrote:

My ability to be an effective communicator in dealing with employees, management, and outside parties is the strength of my financial leadership. My experience and skills will enable me to make a valuable contribution to the Massachusetts Education Association as Chief Financial Officer, and it would also be gratifying to be able to support and be a part of the Massachusetts public school system. Having attended Massachusetts public schools through graduation from high school, and having four children enrolled in the Brighton School District ranging from kindergarten to grade twelve, I have firsthand knowledge of the importance and quality of our public school system.

Here's the cover letter that got Rich his interview:

Richard M. Cash, CPA
1700 Commonwealth Avenue
Boston, MA 02111
(617) 555-0111

June 10, 1997

Manager of Personnel
Massachusetts Education Association
Kennedy Plaza, Suite 1800
Boston, MA 02155

Dear Manager of Personnel:

My experience includes twenty-two years in financial management, with proven expertise in administering financial policies and procedures, investing and cash management, computer systems, budgeting, tax compliance and financial reporting. I am please to have the opportunity to apply for your position as Chief Financial Officer.

Highlights of my experience include:

- Managed the accounting, tax, cash management, data processing, risk management, records, payroll and administrative services functions.
- Administered human resource needs including salary administration, selection, training and evaluation for staff of 35.
- Developed customized software applications for improved budgeting, investment analysis, revenue and expense accrual and cost-accounting.
- Designed and implemented accounting procedures and controls for cash processing, investments and computer systems.

My ability to be an effective communicator in dealing with employees, management, and outside parties is the strength of my financial leadership. My experience and skills will enable me to make a valuable contribution to the Massachusetts Education Association as Chief Financial Officer, and it would also be gratifying to be able to support and be a part of the Massachusetts public school system. Having attended Massachusetts public schools through graduation from high school, and having four children enrolled in the Brighton School District ranging from kindergarten to grade twelve, I have firsthand knowledge of the importance and quality of our public school system.

I would appreciate the opportunity to discuss in greater detail the contribution I would make to the Massachusetts Education Association. Please contact me at (617) 555-0111 to arrange a meeting.

Sincerely,

Richard M. Cash

Richard M. Cash, CPA

Interestingly, in a little over a month after beginning his job search, Rich got this interview. A couple weeks later he started the new job. A few weeks went by, and another association had finally sorted through all the applicants and called to interview him. With only a few weeks at his new job, he was reluctant to go to the interview. He liked his new position and the people he worked with. I encouraged him to go and investigate this option. He did, but quickly decided he was very happy with the new position he had accepted with the education association, so he declined a second interview with the other employer.

CHLOE—

Her challenge was to write a resumé and cover letter for the job of her dreams.

This client, Chloe, had thought about looking for a new challenge for quite a while. Nothing motivated her until she saw this little ad in the paper:

GRANT ADMINISTRATOR
L.L. BEAN
A sporting goods retailer needs administrator for its foundation. Send resumés.

Chloe loved the outdoors. Hiking and camping were two of her favorite activities. But she had no resumé and hadn't written a cover letter in eight years.

Chloe really had a strong background for the job. In my estimation she was a "good fit." So we created her resumé and cover letter specifically to apply for this job.

Chloe Programs

330 Berry Street
Durham, NH 77777
(616) 555-0111

CAREER OBJECTIVE: **Grant Administrator**

SUMMARY OF QUALIFICATIONS

Six years of management and decision-making responsibility overseeing $500,000+ annual grant program with extensive nonprofit 501(c)(3) organization management and compliance experience. Authority to award 250 grants annually. Ability to effectively analyze and evaluate high volume of written proposals annually. Skilled at working closely with 21-member Board of Directors, individual, at the committee level and on major presentations. Ability to produce large volumes of high quality work using minimum resources. Proven public speaking, training, community relations skill.

PROFESSIONAL EXPERIENCE

Assistant Director, The Commission for the Humanities, Boston, MA, 1987-Present

Grant Administration

- Manage grant program of $500,000+, monitor 300 grants annually including evaluation of grant program.
- Make recommendations to fund or not fund large grants for final board approval on 20+ grants annually. Full authorization of small grant distribution, 250 annually. Evaluate over 400 written proposals per year.
- Written 12 grants to unsolicited and specified grant programs with 80% funded.
- Responsible for compliance on 501(c)(3) regulations, taxes, policies, budget management. Fiscal management.
- Active, contributing member on 21-member Board of Directors.
- Develop/publish grant guidelines/application forms to reflect giving priorities.
- Strategic planning with board to determine giving priorities, long term goals.

Public Relations

- Editor, *Humanities Today,* quarterly magazine.
- Community relations and PR liaison, attending conferences and public meetings to communicate to public the mission of the Commission.
- Published articles, contributed to annual reports. Numerous reports to board, public.
- Press releases, interviewed and quoted by press on work of Commission.
- Coordinate annual public conference.

Communications

- Numerous public presentations on commission. Conference moderator, panelist.
- Instructor, grant writing course, two-day workshop, 40-50 participants, twice annually.
- Computer: IBM proficient, WordPerfect, databases for grant management.

EDUCATION

Bachelor of Arts, German Literature, Wheaton College, MA, 1982
Linguistics/Translation Certificate, University of Munich, Germany, 1985

INTERESTS

Mountain Climbing and Hiking (locally), U.S., Europe, China, Himalayas Backcountry
Skiing, Kayaking, Mountain Biking, Local Sports

Here's Chloe's Power Impact Technique™ cover letter:

Chloe Programs
330 Berry Street
Durham, NH 03264
(616) 555-0111

February 16, 1997

L.L. Bean
PO Box 1938
Sportsland, Maine 01133
Attn: SE 1794

Dear L.L. Bean:

Six years of management and decision-making responsibility overseeing $500,000+ annual grant program for a private, nonprofit 501(c)(3) organization, The Commission for the Humanities, has given me extensive skills in the field of grant making, including:

- Ability to analyze and evaluate high volumes of written grant applications
- Monitor 300 grant awards annually
- Coordinate grant making activities with a 21-member Board of Directors
- Authorize distribution of 250 grants annually
- Publish a quarterly magazine
- Collaborate on strategic planning
- Develop and conduct public outreach programs
- Work effectively with high productivity using minimal resources
- Teach grant writing classes

The focus of The Commission for the Humanities grant making program is to increase public awareness and understanding of issues related to education, the arts, healthcare, the environment, social issues, social welfare, science and technology.

I believe these abilities coupled with the experience in several focused areas of grant making will bring great value to your Grant Administrator position. I would enjoy the opportunity to discuss them with you in greater detail. Please contact me at (616) 555-0111 to arrange a meeting.

Your time and consideration are greatly appreciated.

Sincerely,

Chloe Programs

Chloe Programs

Notice the important points—the strong opening was essential, as we knew this ad would draw hundreds and hundreds of responses.

Her bulleted statements were short but effective:

✔ Ability to analyze and evaluate high volumes of written grant applications.

✔ Monitor 300 grant awards annually.

✔ Authorize distribution of 250 grants annually.

✔ Publish a quarterly magazine.

✔ Develop and conduct public outreach programs.

✔ Teach grant writing classes.

Today, Chloe's still at L.L. Bean. I hear through the grapevine that they really love her there. She's found a great place to work and a job that's proven to be the perfect fit for her.

SAM—

His challenge was to return to work after a three-year sabbatical.

In our employers' survey, 80% found work gaps "worrisome." So I chose a special case for my last example. This client, Sam, was in the highly structured world of accounting. He had done something that his peers had deemed would be professional suicide: He took a three-year sabbatical from work. He traveled, went on several medical relief missions, and enjoyed life. When I met him, the money was close to running out, so he was job hunting with no success. Sam faced a big obstacle.

Although only three of our surveyed hiring managers said they would completely dismiss a candidate after one year of unemployment, most of the others told us they'd want a "reasonable explanation." A "sabbatical" as Sam called it, would hardly be easily accepted in the finance world. I'm telling Sam's story because he faced what many colleagues told him were insurmountable odds as he began to look for a new position. Together we wrote a good resumé that focused on his past skills, while keeping the sabbatical toward the end in his work history. He had accomplished much before he left, but the gap would be impossible to totally hide.

Samuel Sabbatical, CPA

21135 32nd Ave. S.
Detroit, MI 71111
(714) 555-6100

CAREER OBJECTIVE: **Accounting Manager**

SUMMARY OF QUALIFICATIONS

Seventeen years in accounting management with proven track record and expertise in streamlining and directing accounting operations. Able to efficiently reorganize/reengineer processes and procedures to increase efficiency, accuracy, and internal control. Strengths lie in team development, productivity increases, and excellent interpersonal communications skills.

PROFESSIONAL EXPERIENCE

Administration Manager, General Motors, Flint, MI, 1978-1991
(Promoted from General Accounting Manager, Cost Accounting Manager, Assistant to Controller)

Accounting

- 13 years in accounting management for large manufacturer, duties included: G/L, A/P, A/R, fixed assets, payroll, taxes, budgeting, forecasting, financial procedures, internal control.
- Represented employer in state tax hearing. Successful defense. Result: $200,000+ tax savings.
- Reorganized fifteen person department, streamlined procedures, eliminated redundancy, and reengineered reporting system. Six positions eliminated. Annual cost savings: $150,000+.
- Managed three cost-accounting systems: standard, process, job cost. Analyzed and adjusted cost standards and overhead rates. Audited sales contracts from $100,000–$5 million.
- Planned and executed the physical inventory involving 100+ employees. Results were procedural changes that minimized write-offs and strengthened inventory control.
- Managed internal control program. Oversaw the evaluation and testing of operating and financial departments. Redesigned procedures to increase productivity/accuracy, eliminate redundancies, avoid excess expenditures, and safeguard assets.

Administration/Personnel

- Recruited/hired key financial people who proved to be outstanding, 100% were promoted.
- Trained financial managers and staff on accounting procedures, computer and hiring skills.
- Educated division managers on effective internal controls. Trained division operational and financial staff on how to audit/evaluate internal control systems.

Computer Skills

- IBM PC and mainframe experience with expertise utilizing Lotus, Excel, WordPerfect, databases and spreadsheets. Provided staff training on Lotus.
- Converted 150+ corporate manager expense accounting system into a streamlined, well documented, computerized system. Increased productivity, reduced staff requirements 50%.

WORK HISTORY

Sabbatical Leave, World travel/medical relief work in Central America, 7/92-12/94
General Accounting Manager, Cost Accounting Manager, Assistant to the Controller,
Administrative Manager, Accounting Supervisor, General Motors,
Flint, MI, 1979-1992
Controller, Timber Homes, Kent, MI, 1977-1979
Assistant Controller, Unlimited Sportswear, Detroit, MI, 1975-1977
Auditor, Arthur Anderson, Detroit, MI, 1974-1975

EDUCATION

M.B.A., University of Illinois, Urbana, Illinois, 1974
B.A., Accounting and Finance majors, DePaul University, 1969

Here's Sam's letter that we created for the accounting manager opening at Upjohn:

Samuel Sabbatical, CPA

21135 32nd Ave. S.

Detroit, MI 71111

(714) 555-6100

June 1, 1997

Upjohn

Attention: Bill Williamson

Box 662

Kalamazoo, MI 49000

Dear Bill:

Proven experience managing the general ledger and financial reporting for a large manufacturer, liaison responsibility for foreign operations, plus management of the accounting procedures and the internal control program is the expertise I'd bring to your International Accounting Control Manager position at Upjohn.

Highlights of my experience include:

- Over four years experience in managing the general ledger and financial reporting for a major division of General Motors, plus consolidate financial statements and foreign currency translations.
- Accounting liaison responsibilities for foreign divisions including those with controllers for whom English is a second language. I speak conversational Spanish.
- Management of the division's internal control programs including: reviewing and reengineering procedures to enhance financial and operational control, and educating division managers on effective internal controls.
- Management of the division's billing and accounts receivable, accounts payable, fixed assets and hourly payroll. Managed a staff of fourteen.
- Annual and semi-annual budgets, monthly profit forecasts and cash flow forecasting.
- Strong PC and mainframe computer experience with expertise utilizing Windows, Lotus, Excel and WordPerfect. Excellent communication and interpersonal skills.

I would like to discuss in greater detail the valuable contributions I could bring to the Upjohn team. Please contact me at (714) 555-0111 to arrange a meeting.

Sincerely,

Samuel Sabbatical

Samuel Sabbatical, CPA

This letter got a screening phone call from personnel. Today, many employers call to inquire about qualifications with the set goal of disqualifying candidates. In Sam's case, he used the conversation to learn more about the job, and he was quite savvy in writing a follow-up letter that truly pointed out some valuable skills the employer could use. He wrote the following letter:

Samuel Sabbatical, CPA
21135 32nd Avenue South
Detroit, MI 71111
(714) 555-6100

June 14, 1997

Mr. Joe Brownstone
Upjohn Co.
Box 662
Kalamazoo, MI 49000

Dear Mr. Brownstone:

Thank you for the telephone call late Wednesday afternoon regarding the position of International Accounting Manager with Upjohn. Upon reflecting on our discussion and reviewing the description advertised in the newspaper, I believe that there are some key strengths that I can bring to the position that we did not discuss or discussed only briefly.

My experience appears to provide a very good fit with the responsibilities described for the position of International Accounting Control Manager for the following reasons:

- I have eight years experience as a manager with General Motors. I have managed accounts payable and cash disbursements, billing and accounts receivable, fixed assets, and state and local taxes.

- As General Accounting Manager for a large General Motors division for more than four years, I was responsible for general ledger operations and financial reporting. I am very comfortable with the monthly closing process and the demands for timely accurate reporting. Division financials were required to be finalized and submitted for consolidation by noon on the sixth workday of the month. Under my supervision this schedule was consistently met month in and month out. All problems, if any, occurring during closing were addressed and solved without jeopardizing the closing schedule.

- I have extensive experience in financial analysis. Along with responsibility for monthly closings came the responsibility for providing both division and corporate management with an analysis of the financial results and a detailed explanation why the results varied from the operating plan. Often, to discover the underlying reasons for variances, I worked on the analysis with the managers of other departments.

- My duties also required the preparation and submission of formal monthly profitability forecasts. Often these were required two or more times a month.

- I am experienced with international operations. As Assistant Controller for Unlimited Sportswear, I had the responsibility for consolidating Canadian and Mexican operations. This included foreign currency translations. I traveled to the Mexican plant to review the financial operations and emphasize the required procedures and controls. As Administrative Manager for General Motors, I was responsible for monitoring and recommending changes to the production mix for trucks manufactured in Brazil. I was in frequent contact with the Brazilian manufacturer.

- I was responsible for the internal control program for my division. Under this program, all operating and financial functions were formally audited on a one to three year schedule, depending on the risk assigned to each area. The internal control assessments were performed under my supervision. The results were reported to division and corporate management. I trained department heads on the principles of good internal control and helped them develop and implement revised procedures to strengthen existing controls.

- Recruiting, training and developing staff into motivated, productive teams is a strength that I am particularly proud of. When training, I not only explain the procedure but the reason for the procedure and how it fits into the overall company operations. I have managed departments as large as fifteen people. Most of my career has included supervisory responsibility.

- I possess strong PC and mainframe computer skills with expertise utilizing Windows, Lotus, Excel and WordPerfect.

Please contact me at (714) 555-6100 to discuss in greater detail the valuable contributions I can bring to the Upjohn team.

Sincerely,

Samuel Sabbatical

Samuel Sabbatical, CPA

Very few people ever take this extra step. It worked and got Sam the interview. We practiced answers to questions and created his 60 Second Sell and 5 Point Agenda (interview concepts discussed in my book *24 Hours to Your Next Job, Raise, or Promotion,* Wiley). Sam was really ready for the big event. After the interview Sam wrote again, this time with a very influential follow-up thank-you letter.

Samuel Sabbatical, CPA
21135 32nd Avenue South
Detroit, MI 71111
(714) 555-6100

July 6, 1997

Mr. Ken Deverall
Upjohn Co.
Box 662
Kalamazoo, MI 49000

Dear Mr. Deverall:

Thank you for the opportunity to discuss with you the position of International Accounting Control Manager for Upjohn. We covered a lot of ground in the three hours we spent together. The Upjohn environment in the international division is certainly interesting because of its complexities.

I am effective in operating in complex environments. General Motors is a large organization with thirty cost centers. As General Accounting Manager, I am accustomed to reviewing the general ledger each day during closing to identify errors and omissions in the ledger. Under my supervision, the closing process was completed on time, at noon on the sixth workday, month in and month out, without exception. I also performed financial analysis of the financial statements after closing was completed. As Cost Accounting Manager, I also dealt with a complex environment. I was responsible for three different cost-accounting systems: standard costs for the winch product line; job costs for rail cars and industrial products; and process costs for foundry products.

I am a specialist in internal control. I managed the General Motors internal control program for three years. This program formally assessed the internal controls in place for each financial and operating function (such as cash, general ledger, and purchasing) on a one to three year schedule, depending on the risk assigned to each area. These assessments were performed under my supervision. I advised the assessment teams when they encountered problems. I reengineered procedures to improve internal controls. I also presided over the meetings with department heads discussing the results of the assessments. Assessment findings were reported to division and corporate management.

Ken, from our meeting, I feel that we share a common business philosophy and I believe that I can work effectively with you to bring about the improvements you outlined. I look forward to discussing with you in greater detail the positive contributions I can bring to your team. Please call me at (714) 555-6100.

Sincerely,

Samuel Sabbatical

Samuel Sabbatical, CPA

We later learned his letters really impressed and influenced this employer. They brought to light his abilities and kept reinforcing that he could do the job. It also appeared he had not "lost it" while he was on his sabbatical. The letters helped relieve any doubts the employer may have had. His extra letters were indeed powerful and highly effective for a man whom critics said would never land another prominent position in his field again.

Summary

Powerful cover letters really make an impression. They can make the difference from being "one in the stack" to "one to call in for an interview." In our survey of over 600 hiring managers, nearly every respondent selected The Power Impact Technique letters as their preferred style. It's so concise and content-driven—that's what gets attention.

I used real-life clients who all faced situations you may encounter. Everyone had the same thing happen—they got hired! Mary wrote only one letter! Diane was able to change into a new career she loves. Joan left all her discouragement behind when her letter sailed to the top of 265 others, helping her get a terrific new job after she was fired, no less. Rich's termination and expectation of a one-year search was quickly cut off when his second letter got him that special interview. Chloe went after her dream job, and one letter later she, too, was hired! Sam took a sabbatical to enjoy the world and silenced the naysayers by landing a fabulous job after a three-year hiatus.

All these clients, and hundreds more, found success using The Power Impact Technique. Now *your* success using your own attention-getting cover letters lies just ahead!

MORE SUCCESSFUL COVER LETTERS

4

Every one of these cover letters at the very least landed an interview—most applicants got the jobs! To guide you, I've selected letters that cover many potential situations: promotions, similar positions, career changing, utilizing volunteer work, leaving the military, and so forth. I've written comments to point out important insights that can aid you as you consider your own skills, experiences, and talents. Lee, an executive recruiter who's helped clients hire hundreds of executives, said: "Use your cover letter to tell me what you can offer my company that makes you special. Why do I want to bring you in for an interview over the hundreds of other candidates we're considering." Larry Tomon, a senior executive at Symmetrical Technologies, tells us: "Give details on what strengths will be delivered to successfully fulfill the job requirements. I want specific accomplishments." Once you've thoroughly read these letters you'll see the dramatic results of using The Power Impact Technique.

I've included some want ads and identified both the NOTED and ASSUMED needs. Look over the commentary, the job analysis, and the proven examples. You'll see how effective The Power Impact Technique truly is. With the first few letters, I've taken the liberty of providing the actual want ad. I've stressed their key points and then identified the employer's NOTED needs and ASSUMED needs, and I follow with the actual letter that the client used.

Proven Cover Letter Examples

BARBARA—
Vice president of administration position

JOB ANALYSIS AND LETTER

Here's the job announcement that ran in the *Wall Street Journal* that caught Barbara's attention:

> **VICE PRESIDENT OF ADMINISTRATION** needed for international consulting group. Challenging opportunity for successful executive with proven track record in creating systems, policies and procedures to help a top industry leader like us excel.
>
> In exchange for a higher than average salary, we are looking for ten years experience, human resource responsibility over 75 or more employees, superior computer systems skills and expertise in re-engineering and TQM systems. A strong communicator with formal presentation skills a must.
>
> Send letter of interest to: Box 55555, *The Wall Street Journal.*

Now this is a tough one. Whenever it's a blind ad (you don't know who the employer is), it requires more effort on your part to try to decipher the true needs and assumed skills. Blind ads typically get 50% fewer responses than want ads with noted employers, but since most *Wall Street Journal* ads are blind, they often attract a higher percentage of responses.

We began by writing out the NOTED NEEDS:

1. VP level—10 years experience
2. International consulting group
3. Track record creating systems policies and procedures
4. HR responsibility over 75+ employees
5. Computer systems expertise
6. Reengineering and TQM experience

We also sketched out the ASSUMED NEEDS:

1. Development of employee accountability and productivity
2. Utilization and implementation of leading-edge technology

Here's The Power Impact Technique letter that Barbara sent:

Barbara Wheeler
14701 212nd Ave
Ft Worth, TX 75251
(214) 555-0111

March 22, 1997

Box 55555
The Wall Street Journal
1233 Regal Row
Dallas, TX 75247

To Whom It May Concern:

Fifteen years experience as Director of Administration for an internationally reimbursed consulting organization with expertise in all facets of internal operations and administration including the development of policy and procedure to create efficient systems and processes, plus the development of employee accountability and productivity is the experience I'd bring to your position of Vice President of Administration.

As a part of top management, I currently manage administrative operations for an office of fifty professionals and twenty-five support staff. Major responsibilities include:

- Hiring of 150 plus employees.
- Development of a large technical library.
- Created a sophisticated automated records management system.
- Established a micro support department serving two hundred users in a Local Area Network (LAN) environment.
- Oversee a large word-processing and reprographics department and an internal accounting department.
- Successfully implemented leading edge technology in all departments to increase productivity and efficiency.
- Trained in Total Quality Management (TQM) techniques to develop continuous process improvement in office systems.

I interact well with staff and clients at all levels and have been active in representing my organization in several high-level community elected and appointed positions. I have made numerous persuasive presentations to city, county, and state government agencies and legislators and have been an effective negotiator and administrator in these roles.

I would like to meet with you to discuss the valuable contribution I might make to your organization's success.

Sincerely,

Barbara Wheeler

Barbara Wheeler

This letter stood out from over 1,000 others—she got the interview.

This ad drew unbelievable competition: over 1,000 responses! In fact, the recruiting process took over two months, and Barbara had "forgotten" about this job when this company's recruiter called. She had a screening interview and was impressed with both the job and the company. The ad did not mention the job's location or the fact that extensive travel would be required. Barbara did very well in the first interview. In the end, Barbara refused the company's offer to fly back in for a final interview. She decided after her first visit that she did not want to move to Delaware. It was a difficult decision, since the company offered a terrific salary and overseas travel that very much appealed to her.

It's nice to know that you can always refuse a job, or interview in this case, if it's not a great fit in every aspect for you.

BILL—
Business Development Specialist Position

JOB ANALYSIS AND LETTER

Bill saw a small ad that was a part of a large computer hardware company's Sunday advertisement. It listed two possibilities:

Account Executives   BA/BS essential—MBA preferred
                          Strong technical knowledge

Business Developers

Not much to go on. In fact, Bill had tried to answer this ad three or four months earlier with no response. I suggested he call the company and ask if they had a job description. They did and agreed to fax it. Here's what he received:

BUSINESS DEVELOPMENT SPECIALIST (BDS)—
SYSTEMS INTEGRATION
JOB DESCRIPTION

The Business Development specialist works closely with the Delivery Unit Manager(s) in their assigned territory. Their role is selling and marketing SI Services. The primary goal of the BDS is the achievement of the PSC Unit's financial goals.

BDS responsibilities include: Identifying, qualifying, and driving profitable new SI business opportunities in support of sales, channels, and new customers. Participation in the account planning process. Developing, implementing, and managing a business development plan. Coordinating local demand creation activities. Supporting corporate programs at the local level building, maintaining, and managing excellent customer account relationships. Assisting in the development of work statements and proposals based on customer expectations and delivery capacity.

Note: Travel up to 30%

Working from the job description, Bill identified these employer NOTED NEEDS:

1. Program management and marketing of systems information

2. Sales and new business development experience

3. Technical, consulting support to potential customers

We discussed the position and realized that the ASSUMED NEEDS were:

1. Proven track record of success

Here's The Power Impact Technique letter that got Bill an interview:

Bill landed this job with a better salary and more responsibility.

William Monroe
49 Lowell Drive
Natick, MA 02161
(617) 555-0111

August 20, 1996

Digital Equipment Corporation
Department 036 ACI
500 108th Avenue N.E.
Framingham, MA 02180

Reference: Business Development Specialist position advertised.

I have spent the past five years as a Customer Program Manager directly managing the marketing, development, and implementation of a new software application for a customer information system at a Fortune 100 company. I have extensive experience in business management, software systems development, and technical product sales and marketing. My strengths lie in my communication skills, analytical abilities, technical expertise, and in my ability to build cohesive teams.

Using an end-user approach, I have led a cross-functional team in the development and implementation of a new concept resulting in a client/server application that our customers access worldwide, 24 hours a day, 7 days a week. As Program Manager, I am the primary customer interface, responsible for defining system requirements, work statement development, and project resource acquisition and planning. The resulting application and information system have greatly reduced communication cycle time, enabling shorter product order-to-delivery cycles, and has tremendously increased customer satisfaction.

In spite of the current downsizing activity at my present company, I have managed to obtain continuous funding for this project by demonstrating rapid payback periods and persistent development progress with limited resources.

I have experience in business process redesign, analyzing and recommending business process improvements for our customers, as well as within my current employer. As an account manager, I was the technical interface to our customers, responsible for identifying and managing technical and business customer requirements.

Enclosed is my resumé for your consideration. I would like to discuss how I may contribute my skills in the referenced position to increase the sales of Digital's products and services. I look forward to hearing from you. Thank you for your time and thoughtful consideration.

Sincerely,

William Monroe

William Monroe

TOM—
Human resources position

JOB ANALYSIS AND LETTER

Tom had just completed a graduate program in human resources when this small ad caught his eye:

> **HUMAN RESOURCES** professional wanted to work for Catholic Community Services, a large nonprofit organization with 700 employees. A generalist background and two years experience is desired. Send resumés to:
>
> Catholic Community Services
> PO Box 1111
> St. Louis, MO 63110

Again, not too much to go on. The employer's NOTED NEEDS were:

1. Two years experience in various areas within a human resource department

ASSUMED NEEDS:

1. Experience in the benefits area within an HR company

2. Hands-on expertise with the HR computer system

3. Degree in HR

4. Diverse employee exposure

5. Training skills

Note that Tom wasn't sure, but feared hiring would be a major need of this employer. Since he had no experience in that area, he excluded mentioning it in his letter.

Here's The Power Impact Technique letter that opened the door for Tom:

Tom Greene
4322 Grand Blvd. S.
St. Louis, MO 63107
(314) 555-0111

May 12, 1996

Catholic Community Services
PO Box 1111
St. Louis, MO 63110

Re: Human Resource Position

Working executive in a fast-paced Human Resource department, comprehensive problem-solving skills in a dynamic environment, and excellent oral and written communication skills is the background I would bring to your HR position. My history includes:

- Providing customer service in the Benefits Section of a Human Resources department including new employee benefits' orientation, enrollment in benefits programs and troubleshooting employee's concerns.
- Hands-on experience with two Human Resource Information Systems.
- Ability to work with a diverse populations at all levels of an organization.
- Graduate work in Human Resources management with knowledge and experience with HR laws and programs including ADA, FMLA, EEOC.
- Presentation of training on skills enhancement and increasing personal effectiveness, locally and at statewide professional conferences.

The enclosed resumé will give you additional information on my training and experience. I would like an opportunity to meet discuss the openings further. I can be reached at (314) 555-0111. Your time and consideration is appreciated.

Sincerely,

Tom Greene

Tom Greene

Tom landed this terrific job that he desperately wanted.

CANDICE—
Administrative services manager position

JOB ANALYSIS AND LETTER

Candice wanted the job at this prestigious company so badly she could taste it. Terrific company, one with growth, was exactly where she wanted to move. Here's the ad she'd found posted at the city library:

Location: Administrative Services Department; Carillon Point, Kirkland

Position: ADMINISTRATIVE SERVICES MANAGER

Responsibilities:
- Manage the Administrative Services Group for Sprint Cellular Communications, Inc. Corporate Headquarters. Areas of function responsibility include: Receptionist, Mailroom, Copy Center, General Office Management and Facilities Planning for our current space in Carillon Point and two buildings in the Plaza at Yarrow Bay (occupancy to take place late September, 1993 and mid March, 1994).
- Corporate Headquarters presently houses approximately 350 persons, including 50 consultants. The Administrative Services manager's duties will include maintaining relationships with the landlords for all tenant services, negotiating with vendors for office services, and managing day-to-day building operations.
- Initially supervise a staff of six, with added personnel as expansion occurs in the Plaza at Yarrow Bay.
- The position will require significant efforts in space planning and coordinating the locations, and remodeling in Carillon Point.

Qualifications:
- Excellent communication, staff development, organization, planning, and negotiation skills.
- Prior management experience.
- Strong sense of team building.
- Ability to deal with multiple landlords.
- Ability to work independently in a dynamic high-technology environment.

Please send resumé and cover letter specifying the position desired to:

People Development Department
Sprint Corporation
Box 5400
Shawnee Mission, KS 66205

Candice knew that this was a rapidly emerging company and very progressive.

The NOTED NEEDS were:

1. Management of administrative services

2. Landlord/vendor dealings

3. Negotiating contracts

4. Space planning and construction build out

5. Excellent communication and organizational skills

ASSUMED NEEDS:

1. Recruited, hired, and developed staff

2. Experience in a fast-growing company

Here's The Power Impact Technique letter that got her the interview:

Candice Frasier
10322 Metcalf
Overland Park, KS 66212
(913) 555-0111

Candice got the interview.

March 22, 1993

People Development Department
Sprint Corporation
Box 5400
Shawnee Mission, KS 66205
Subject: ADMINISTRATIVE SERVICES MANAGER

People Development:

Versatile Administration Manager with ten years of proven expertise in office administration, space allocation, planning, construction, contract negotiations, financial operations, computer systems, with emphasis on staff development within a rapidly expanding company briefly summarizes the background I'd bring to your Administrative Services Manager position. Highlights of my experience include:

- Established office administration for 3 rapidly expanding international companies including: office layout, construction, personnel needs analysis, hiring, purchasing, computer network, telecommunications, policies, procedures, budgets, forecasts.
- Corporate project manager of $1.3 million office and laboratory construction including negotiations, construction meetings, compliance auditing, and financial review resulting in $200,000 savings.
- Tough contract negotiator on 400+ contracts/deals with vendors and bankers.
- Landlord/Tenant liaison successfully resolving conflicts, problems, issues with efficient, speedy compliance.
- Recruited, hired and developed staff into a motivated highly productive team.
- Personally hired over 50 individuals.

My excellent communication skills have added to my success in dealing effectively with a diverse and international clientele. I enjoy challenges and using my analytical and organizational skills to aid my employer in rapid business expansion. I know my resourcefulness has repeatedly benefited my employers in the past.

I would like to discuss in greater detail the valuable contribution I would make as a part of Sprint's team. I can be reached at (913) 555-0111 to arrange a meeting. Your consideration is most appreciated.

Sincerely,

Candice Frasier

Candice Frasier

Candice was very disappointed when she left that interview. The job was not at a higher level of responsibility or salary that she was seeking. She declined a second interview and later went on to open her own company.

TRACY—

Program director position

JOB ANALYSIS AND LETTER

Tracy was hoping to move to the West Coast. She had outstanding qualifications for this job. But the cost of relocation was sure to negatively impact her candidacy. Since another peer encouraged her to apply, she knew her letter must focus on the results she had achieved at her current continuing education department to get serious consideration. Here's the ad as it appeared in her association journal:

DIRECTOR OF CONTINUING LEGAL EDUCATION

The California State Bar Association is seeking candidates for the position of Director of the CLE Department. The Director supervises a staff of 18 reports to the Executive Director/CEO, and has budget responsibilities of approximately $9,600,000.

The successful candidate for this position will have significant experience in adult continuing education, along with strong management, organization, programming, financial, and marketing skills. A law degree or legal experience is preferred, not required.

The CSBA has approximately 70,000 active members and a staff of 90+. The position offers excellent benefits and a salary commensurate with qualifications and experience. Please submit resumés including salary requirements to:

Deidre Templeton, HR Manager
CSBA—500 Westin Building
20001 Sixth Avenue,
Los Angeles, CA 90015

CSBA is an Equal Opportunity Employer. The deadline for submitting applications is February 23, 1997. All communications will be treated on a confidential basis.

The NOTED NEEDS were:

1. Supervise staff of eighteen

2. Significant experience in continuing adult education

3. Strong management, programming, financial, and marketing skills

4. Law degree preferred (*did not have*)

The ASSUMED NEEDS:

1. Program development

2. Innovative programs that succeeded

3. Increasing attendance and revenues

4. Stellar performer in past job

Tracy and I were not concerned that she lacked a law degree. We predicted they would have hundreds of lawyers with little meeting planning experience apply. They did. They also had over 100 qualified association executives competing for this highly paid, coveted position.

Here's The Power Impact Technique letter that Tracy sent:

Tracy Blacke, CMP
777 W. 57th Ave. #633
New York, NY 10022
(212) 555-0111

February 9, 1997

Mr. Dennis Hellman, Executive Director
California State Bar Association
500 Westin Building
2001 Sixth Avenue
Los Angeles, CA 90015

Dear Mr. Hellman:

At John Edenbaugh's urging, I'd like to have you consider my application for your Director of Continuing Legal Education position. To familiarize you a little better, let me highlight some of my qualifications:

- I have eight years directing the continuing professional education program for the New York Medical Association.
- Doubled annual revenues from $2.9 to $6.1 million.
- Increased profitability by 30%.
- Increased course offerings and delivery methods resulting in a significant increase in member satisfaction.
- Recognized as one of the top five associations in the United States.
- Winner of numerous awards and professional honors including *National Meeting Planner of the Year* and recently served as the President of the American Society of Association Executives.

I would like to discuss with you and the committee the valuable contributions I'd bring to the California State Bar Association. I can be reached at (212) 555-0111.

Sincerely,

Tracy Blacke, CMP

Tracy Blacke, CMP

**Tracy landed the job
with a $10,000 bonus.**

Tracy flew out for an interview on Thursday and was called to come back in on Friday before she caught a plane back home. She was quite surprised to be offered the job and immediately was thrown into salary negotiations. A $10,000 signing bonus covered her relocation expenses, and she raves about it never snowing in southern California.

MARILYN—

Shopping center manager position

JOB ANALYSIS AND LETTER

Marilyn was thrilled to see this ad, as most real estate management positions had dried up as the local economy cooled off. Before we met she'd sent off over 100 cover letters to no avail. She was way overqualified for most of these positions. Her old letter also lacked the facts regarding the results she'd achieved in her past positions. She was excellent at her job, but she wrote a poor generic cover letter. A friend had recommended I help her.

Our first step was to analyze the ad:

SHOPPING CENTER MANAGER

One of the nation's largest shopping center development companies has an immediate opening for a manager. Candidate should have a BA Degree with excellent verbal and written communication skills. Should have previous experience in retail, property management or related field.

For prompt consideration send resumé and salary history in confidence to:

Box D608
Miami Herald
P O Box 91019
Miami, FL 41114

Not much was listed for the NOTED NEEDS:

1. Degree

2. Previous experience

Therefore, we spent some time analyzing the job based on what she'd done at her last position. Here's what we came up with for ASSUMED NEEDS:

1. Proven experience managing large-scale shopping centers

2. Merchant launches

3. Produced results (i.e., increasing sales and profitability)

4. Coordinated special events and merchandising promotions

e's Marilyn's Power Impact Technique letter:

...er-
...vas
strictly on salary nego-
tiations) and beat some
of the top real estate
managers in the coun-
try to land this coveted
position.

Marilyn Jessup
47 Independence Dr.
Coral Cables, FL 41134
(305) 555-0111

July 19, 1997

Box D608
Miami Herald
P.O. Box 91019
Miami, FL 41114

Dear Company:

Twelve years producing profitable, measurable results in marketing and shopping center management is the expertise I'd bring to your Shopping Center Manager position.

Highlights of my background include:

- Management of four regional/urban shopping centers, $355 million in annual sales.
- Obtained up to 18% sales growth for upscale, urban shopping center *every year* during seven years mall was in existence.
- Coordinated more than 50 new merchant launches.
- Handled daily operations and crisis management for such disasters as flooding, earthquakes, public relations scares, expediently.
- Organized 300 large-scale special and merchandising events from concept to conclusion.

I would like to discuss in detail the valuable contributions I would bring to your team. I can be reached at (305) 555-0111. Your consideration is most appreciated.

Sincerely,

Marilyn Jessup

Marilyn Jessup

Her letter was very straightforward in bringing out her accomplishments very quickly. "Twelve years experience producing profitable, measurable results . . ." was a very eye-catching lead-in. In the body, she declares, "Obtained 18% sales growth every year," teasing the employer with a fact that surely matters to the owners.

She reports that the job is very demanding and wonderfully fun all at the same time. She shared with me that before this ad, she'd gone almost three months without one solid job lead. These top positions were so few and far between. But—and it's a big *but*—when the opening came, she put all her efforts into preparing the best self-marketing package she could. It just goes to show you—you need only one opportunity.

LAURA—
Public relations position

JOB ANALYSIS AND LETTER

Laura Krupnick wanted a new job in the very crowded field of public relations. She also needed a large company with good benefits and retirement plan. Competition for a public relations job in Chicago was enormous. When Laura heard me on the radio one day, she made a beeline to my seminar sponsored by a local college that night.

After the program, she told me she needed my help in writing a cover letter that would finally get her noticed. Two days later she faxed me this ad:

> **PR SPECIALIST** needed to help increase public recognition of city's recycling program. 5–7 years in PR, advertising or media is required. Experience in special events, PSAs are necessary. Must be postmarked no later than Mar. 1st.
>
> Mail to:
>
> Recycling Program
> City of Chicago, Personnel
> Dexter Horton Building
> Chicago, IL 17931

Laura had noted on the fax that she'd learned from a friend who worked for the city that she really needed to stress her success with local media and events. So with that piece of information, these were the NOTED NEEDS:

1. Five to seven years experience

2. Successful media placements

3. Extensive events coordination

ASSUMED NEEDS:

1. Creating the PSA, marketing and promotion, press releases, brochures, flyers, and pamphlets.

Analysis of Laura's skills brought out one important trait that might matter: She'd often got corporations to underwrite the costs of events, printing, and so forth. This was certainly worth mentioning.

Here's The Power Impact Technique letter that got Laura the interview:

Laura Krupnick

1711 Michigan Ave Apt. 21
Chicago, IL 17933
(312) 555-0111

June 16, 1997

Don Hayes
City of Chicago Personnel
Dexter Horton Bldg.
Chicago, IL 17931

Dear Don:

Over ten years of proven expertise in public relations, media relations, and promotions is the background I'd bring to the City's Recycling Program. Highlights of my experience include:

- Wrote press releases that aired on all three local TV affiliates and numerous radio stations.
- Secured major corporate sponsorships to underwrite program costs or events from Bank of America, United Airlines, and Neiman Marcus.
- Created repeated newspaper publicity generated through press releases and media contacts.
- Produced brochures, booklet, flyers, pamphlets, media releases, PSAs, promotional video, radio commercial, and print advertisements.
- Coordinated 45+ special events, including dinners, receptions, lunches, exhibits, auctions, conferences, concerts, exhibitions. Responsible for planning, lodging, catering, marketing, logistics, publicity, volunteer recruitment, and budgeting.

I would like to discuss in greater detail the valuable contributions I could bring promoting the City's recycling efforts. Please contact me at (312) 555-0111 to arrange a meeting.

Your time and consideration are most appreciated.

Sincerely,

Laura Krupnick

Laura Krupnick

> *Laura landed this and another position in the same week!*

Terrific Job Search Resources and Advice

85% of all jobs are never advertised!

Bonus

By now you may be wondering exactly how people are finding all these job openings. Some were in the newspaper, but others required detective skills. The want ads cover only 7 to 8% of all jobs currently available. Too often, job hunters simply don't know where else to look. Here are some good avenues to pursue.

GO TO THE LIBRARY

Conduct some market research to analyze where the best opportunities lie for you. Your goal is to reach the hiring manager—your potential boss—not the human resources department. Ask the reference librarian to help you locate the following resources, and you'll be on your way finding out about many hidden opportunities. Start out with old newspapers and check the ads—oftentimes people don't work out, so a phone call or sending a prospect letter (in forthcoming chapters) can be quite effective.

Look at annual reports, trade magazines, CD-ROM computerized employer data, trade journals, Yellow Pages and business directories. A couple good ones to check out are *Hoover's Handbook of American Business, Hoover's Master List of America's Top 2,500 Employers, The Thomas Registers, Million Dollar Directory,* as well as *Standard and Poor's Registry of Corporations, Directors and Executives.* Another great library resource is the database system called *Infotrac,* which has reams of information on more than 150,000 companies based on articles from newspapers, magazines, and trade journals.

USE THE INTERNET

The information highway lists thousands and thousands of job openings. The big trick is not spending all your time just looking for them. The best places to look for leads are on a company's web page. These are often found by typing in www.companyname.com (e.g., www.costco.com). There are also many career web sites out there that carry extensive lists of job openings. Be prepared to search out the geographical location and job title you seek, since there is no easy index to do that for you.

Some good web sites to visit include the following:

http://www.espan.com
http://www.jobbankusa.com
http://www.careermosaic.com
http://www.monster.com
http://www.careermag.com
http://www.jobtrak.com/jobguide

You'll want to create a resumé or employer ad about yourself and your qualifications. Post it on bulletin boards and company web sites. For a sample resumé or short online ad, use my book *Winning Resumés,* published by Wiley.

Two-thirds of all jobs are found by obtaining a lead through your contacts.

NETWORK

Ask family, friends, and colleagues for assistance in tracking down people on your list of companies. Be open to adding new companies that they may bring to your attention. Finally, in Chapter 6 of this book, I'll teach you about self-marketing letters—another terrific way to probe openings and get employers' attention.

For more information on looking for a new position, consult my book, *24 Hours to Your Next Job, Raise, or Promotion,* published by Wiley.

Internal Promotions

Applying for a job internally can be tricky. You may know the head of the department that interests you; perhaps you've spoken to that person about the possibilities for employment there.

David had worked for three years inside a very large company in the customer service area. He loved computers and helping people. He called for my assistance when he learned that there might be an internal opening in the technical support area.

We created this friendly letter that was the beginning of his move into the new department. Notice we did not stress most of his current duties, since they had little relationship to being a technical support person. We kept the letter short and friendly—it did the trick. He followed up a few days later with a phone call, and he got the interview.

Here's David's Power Impact Technique letter:

David got the job. He has since been promoted to supervisor of technical support.

David Staden
1 Main Street
City, NY 10036
(201) 555-0111 home
(201) 555-3333 office
e-mail: DSTADEN@viacom.com

June 24, 1996

Ms. Marion Sprouse
712 Avenue of The Americas, Suite 215
New York, NY 10020

Dear Ms. Sprouse:

Over the last three years at Viacom I've excelled in training other department managers and employees on our computer systems and software applications. I'm the person that everyone calls when they can't figure out their computer problem or are having technical difficulties. I really enjoy the technical support aspect of my job and am very interested in moving into a new position where the sole responsibility is technical support and computer training. I'm a very familiar user with all our company's systems and software applications and excel at teaching both technical and non-technical employees alike. I've demonstrated that I have the ability to effectively help people become more productive at their jobs.

I will call you in a couple of days to learn more about your current needs, and the potential opening in your department.

Sincerely,

David Staden

David Staden

Targeting Your Skills to Different Types of Organizations

Corporate cultures differ from each other and can be significantly different from nonprofits or governmental organizations. I've selected these two letters to show how one client using The Power Impact Technique diagnosed the NOTED and ASSUMED needs for the same job at two very different organizations.

JOB ANALYSIS

The first is for a corporation that was rapidly expanding.

NOTED NEEDS:

1. Eight years experience

2. Banking experience

3. Forecasting and budgeting

4. Administration of human resources

5. Computer systems and LAN expertise

ASSUMED NEEDS:

1. Expanding companies need proven, innovative leaders. Hard-core results and analytical strengths must be demonstrated.

You'll notice that we placed Aaron's "CPA" title right after his name. This is an important credential that should be quickly brought to the employer's attention.

This is The Power Impact Technique letter got him the interview:

Aaron Hientz, CPA

1 Main Street
Tulsa, OK 74107
(918) 555-0111

April 21, 1997

Supra Products
Human Resources-CFO
PO Box 3167
Tulsa, OK 74158

Dear Supra,

Ten years in senior financial management with proven expertise in business expansion, well-developed banking relationships, tax accounting, computer systems, costing, and cash management is the background I'd bring to your Controller position.

Highlights of my accomplishments include:

- Extensive forecasting and budgeting expertise, having taken acquisition from $17M–$31M in 24 months.
- Development of comprehensive product sales analysis to identify profit margins, costing, overhead resulting in significant inventory management, cash flow and marketing improvements.
- Administrated human resource functions including: benefits, payroll, employment law, training, worker compensation for staff of 50.
- Installed entire new LAN system for company. Developed custom software programs on invoicing, inventory, costing to maximize productivity.

My ability to be an effective communicator to work with diverse, cross-cultural employees and managers is the strength of my financial leadership. I would like to discuss in greater detail the valuable contributions I would make to Supra. Please contact me at (918) 555-0111 to arrange a meeting.

Your time and consideration is most appreciated.

Sincerely,

Aaron Hientz, CPA

Aaron Hientz, CPA

Interestingly enough, this strong business approach would *not* have worked well for the Kidney Foundation job Aaron also wanted to apply for. A softer, more flowing, personalized manager had to be presented.

The NOTED NEEDS stated:

1. CPA preferred

2. Five to eight years in finance/accounting

3. Computer experience LAN systems

4. Team player

ASSUMED NEEDS:

1. Strong interpersonal skills

Here's The Power Impact Technique letter that also opened the door for Aaron at this nonprofit:

Aaron Hientz, CPA
1 Main Street
Tulsa, OK 74107
(918) 555-0111

August 1, 1997

Midwest Kidney Center
617 Eastlake Ave. E
Tulsa, OK 74123

Dear Midwest Kidney Center:

As a proven financial leader with strengths in strategic planning, accounting management, and team development, please consider the background I'd bring to your Director of Finance position.

As a team developer, I have implemented innovative policies and procedures, changes that streamlined costs and paperwork to maximize productivity. My strength in the computer systems area has been an important asset to my previous employer in which I've automated our entire organization's operations selecting and installing a LAN system. Training others on software applications is my forte.

The radical changes that the healthcare industry faces with managed care and national healthcare require a financial team with good planning skills, plus efficiency that is adaptable to the changing marketplace.

I would like to discuss in greater detail the valuable contributions I'd bring to your financial team development and profitability. I can be reached at (918) 555-0111.

Your consideration is appreciated.

Sincerely,

Aaron Hientz, CPA

Aaron Hientz, CPA

The manufacturing job was the one he really wanted and accepted!

These letters are from the very same person. The tone of each letter is quite different. They stress the strengths that would be important to each organization. Aaron told me he learned a lot from this experience—the necessity to stress how you can meet that specific employer's needs. Aaron had interviews with both employers and left feeling that he could do both jobs well and would succeed in either position.

Referral

Occasionally a friend or colleague known to the employer will tell you about a position. Always use that individual's name to start your letter since it will garner special attention. Keith's colleague told him about a great new opportunity. This referral plus the stated evidence of past success and his management style got him an interview. After two days and six candidates, Keith was offered the job—a position he still holds today.

Alvin's wife actually called an old employer and learned about this job. It was important to show both interest, skills, and a good communication style. He indeed got an interview, but he later turned down this job for another offer that he received. Alvin had been a consultant and used that to aid him in his letter to assure the employer of his strong ability to perform this engineering job. He also pointed out he had been in Kuwait and thus knew what was needed and what he'd be undertaking if he went to Saudi Arabia, where this position was located.

It was a dark day when Kay's boss told her he was letting her go. After a tough weekend, she went straight to work on finding a new position. A former employer told her about this dream job at *Running* Magazine so we got together and created an influential letter to send to their advertising manager.

Keith Whitestone
1 Cobblestone Drive
Short Hills, New Jersey 07078
(201) 555-0111

March 24, 1997

Ms. Melissa Lincoln
ABC Corporation
1700 Jersey Center Plaza
Jersey City, NJ 07310

Dear Ms. Lincoln:

Dave Thomas, President of Metro Cellular, recommended I contact you regarding your search for a CEO, as he is familiar with my strong marketing and finance background and known reputation for developing productive personnel teams within a growing company.

As a company President, I have 10 years of broad based experience which includes product launches, increasing sales profits by 9%, developing complex budgets, establishing solid financial reporting and forecasting systems, as well as performing business/strategic planning.

I believe in words and action that team contributions are an effective way to achieve company goals. Understanding what motivates each staff member to achieve excellence, setting goals and expectation levels for completion with a high degree of proficiency and productivity, supplemented with continual support and leadership achieve job success. I lead by example. I am experienced in evaluating the performance of staff members at various levels to identify both strengths and weaknesses, assist with the establishment of goals, help design strategies to focus efforts on areas requiring improvement, and develop a person's complete understanding of their contribution to the "big picture" and the company's goals as a whole.

I would like to discuss in greater detail my background and the value I would bring to ABC Corporation's team development and profitability. I can be reached at (201) 555-0111.

Sincerely,

Keith Whitestone

Keith Whitestone

Alvin Mayes

27211-200th Street SE
Los Angeles, CA 90038
(213) 555-0111

January 28, 1996

James Rodriguez, HR Director
Saudi Arabia Project
Ralph M. Parsons Company
100 W. Walnut Ave.
Pasadena, CA 91124

Dear Jim,

My wife Mary was pleasantly surprised that you remembered her. Thank you for telling her all about your Saudi Arabia project and, as promised, my resumé is attached.

The projects in Saudi Arabia sound very exciting to me. I bring 15 years of engineering equipment design in the power generation and pipeline areas. Most of my career has been as a consulting engineer. I spent 14 months in Kuwait, thus, I am very familiar with the technical problems and work demands your Saudi Arabia position would require.

To briefly summarize my background, I'd bring 15 years in instrumentation and control equipment design, extensive engineering project management experience, proven troubleshooting expertise, and a track record of streamlining processes and procedures to reduce costs and increase productivity. This is evidenced by the work I did on five power plant designs in which I reduced the man hours by 4100, saving over $100,000.

I would like to discuss in greater detail the valuable contributions I would bring to Parsons, either in Saudi Arabia or on other projects. I do understand these assignments are unaccompanied and I am more than willing to go anywhere I am needed. I can be reached at (213) 555-0111 to arrange a meeting.

Your consideration is most appreciated.

Sincerely,

Alvin Mayes

Alvin Mayes

This employer called her for an interview just minutes after reading her letter.

Kay Quinn
74 East 75th Street, Apt 201
New York, NY 10016
(212) 555-0111

September 14, 1997

Mr. José Gonzales, Advertising Director
Running Magazine
10 Fifth Avenue
New York, NY 10010

Dear Mr. Gonzales:

Tom Norton spoke with you last Friday about the sales and marketing skills I could bring to *Running* magazine. As an avid fan and subscriber of *Running* since 1994, I have given gift subscriptions to my closest friends for the past three years. As a result, most of the recipients have discovered, as have I, what *Running* professes in each issue—*Running* is the most enjoyable way to a lifetime of fitness and good health.

Aside from my overwhelming enthusiasm for *Running* magazine, I have a strong track record in sales, marketing, and public relations, consistently *doubling sales wherever I've worked.* In fact, my employer at the American Medical Journal considered me "among the best sales people he had ever hired." I attribute my success in sales to my proficiency at building relationships and my dedicated follow-through techniques, in conjunction with my ability to listen and understand client needs—the key to satisfied, loyal customers.

Additionally, I have promotion and event planning skills. Last Fall, as my personal commitment to health and my community, I originated a brand new event called "Stride with Pride." In partnership with a local hospital, I planned the program, hired the professional speakers, and obtained the publicity for a 10K race to benefit the National Heart Association. Attendees were treated to a demonstration by Olympic running coach Jacob Stetson and to the inspiring words of Oscar-winning actress Susan Sarandon, who acclaimed the healthy benefits of running. The outstanding result of this event was the creation of a running club that's been going strong ever since.

Mr. Gonzales, I'm already buzzing with a million ideas on how to create more advertising partners and sponsored promotions to increase both revenues and subscribers to *Running* magazine. I'd love to share these ideas with you. My resumé, as well as two letters of recommendation follow. If I don't hear from you before Friday, I'll call you to get a more accurate description of what your current needs might be.

Your consideration and time are most appreciated.

Best Regards,

Kay Quinn

Kay Quinn

Insider Information

So many advertisements leave out the important distinctions of what matters most to employers. Ads and job announcements are often filled with dozens of requirements, where what to stress and what the top priorities are can seem quite unclear. This strategy has worked well for many of my clients. Call the organization and try to discuss the job with the departing manager if possible. Marietta did just that. Her 35-minute phone call (and fast note-taking) allowed her to write a great Power Impact Technique letter that got her an immediate interview five days after she mailed it.

Here's Marietta's Power Impact Technique letter:

Marietta Hudson
417 Big Cattle Drive
Dallas, TX 75241
(214) 555-0111

February 22, 1997

Mr. Palmer
1233 Regal Row
Dallas, TX 75247

Dear Mr. Palmer:

Kate Brown, your departing HR manager, and I have discussed at great length Brookshire Grocery's needs in a Human Resource Manager. Your need for an individual with generalist experience in retail having dealt effectively with unions and upper management who is a contributing part of the executive team—completely describes my background.

I have 19 years' retail, including sales, buyer, merchandiser, and Assistant Store Manager. My last six years were as Human Resource Manager. My experience includes:

- Hiring—recruitment, selection, training, legal compliance, having hired thousands of employees from lowest to top management
- Labor Relations—union contract negotiations, interpretation, implementation, compliance, grievance review over 12 different contracts.
- Administration—streamline and update policies, procedures for over 10,000 employees.
- Employee Relations—one on one counseling, oversee union grievance procedure, conflict resolution, personal issues, and harassment counseling.
- Team Player—Active, vital part of executive team, actively working with departments to achieve company goals, maximize worker productivity to increase profit margins.

I will call you in a few days to arrange a meeting to discuss the valuable contributions I'd make as part of your executive team. Your time and consideration are most appreciated.

Sincerely,

Marietta Hudson

Marietta Hudson

Marietta got an immediate interview.

Volunteer Experience/Reentry

Many women leave the workplace to raise a family. They often choose to return years later, many times because divorce or financial burdens make working a necessity. Too often, women in these circumstances approach me saying, "I need a job. I haven't worked, so I can't offer any experience. Can you help me?"

Elizabeth was one such person. In fact, I often tell people her story and that she said, "I have nothing to sell the employer." She had done volunteer work—a lot of it—but nothing was ever paid. We emphasized what she had done—event planning, fundraising, marketing and promotion, and budget work. Fundraisers, the job Elizabeth was most qualified for, must demonstrate organizational and communication skills. A track record of raising money is helpful to strengthen the appeal of the candidate.

The want ad for this job provided very little information beyond the job title and where to send your resumé. So we covered all the major tasks they were likely to want Elizabeth to do—event planning, solicitation, and marketing—as a part of our job analysis of ASSUMED needs.

No one was more surprised than Elizabeth when this employer called her in for an interview.

Elizabeth Granville
1770 Kirsty Main Drive
Memphis, TN 38138
(901) 555-0111

August 7, 1997

Executive Director
Kellman Blind School
1620 18th Ave.
Memphis, TN 38103

Dear Executive Director,

Fundraising, gift solicitation, event planning with proven expertise in marketing, media relations and strategic planning is the background I'd bring to the position of Development Director.

Highlights of my experience include:

- Coordinated and chaired 3 day national conference, attracted 600 attendees. Budget $100,000. Only conference to make a profit in organization's history.
- Coordinated 55+ special events, including dinners, receptions, lunches, exhibits, auctions, conferences, concerts, exhibitions. Responsible for planning, lodging, catering, marketing, logistics, publicity, volunteer recruitment, and budgeting.
- Budget committee member deciding resource allocations on $3.6 million budget.
- Produced brochures, booklet, flyers, pamphlets, media releases, PSAs, promotional video, radio commercial, print advertisements.

I would like to discuss in greater detail the valuable contributions I could bring to the School. Please contact me at (901) 555-0111 to arrange a meeting.

Your time and consideration are most appreciated.

Sincerely,

Elizabeth Granville

Elizabeth Granville

Elizabeth landed her first paying job at an impressive starting salary.

During my coaching session with Elizabeth, I did point out that she lacked one necessary skill that would tremendously limit her on a job. She had no computer skills at all. I recommended she immediately enroll into two classes: Introduction to Computers and MS Word. She did so the very next day. Eight weeks after that session, she started her new job. She was able to do well and succeed. She told me, "You were right. I would never have made it past day two if I hadn't taken those computer classes. I'm not terrific yet, but I can get by and do my job, and I just love cashing my own paycheck."

Elizabeth is one of the few who realize that sometimes adding a little training to update your skills, plus selling volunteer experience, can result in a $25,000-a-year job right out of the gate. Employers care about experience; whether it's paid or not has little relevance to them, as long as you've done it. So be sure to incorporate associations and civic and community service experience whenever it's relevant to performing the job advertised.

New Graduates

Bachelor's Degree

Getting that first job right out of college can seem nearly impossible when you have little, if any, work experience. Employers worry about your "not yet proven" work ethic or your willingness to stay at their job awhile once they've trained you. College students worry about their lack of experience and seem to think they have no skills to offer an employer. Every student has acquired some skills during his or her college experience. Common ones to point out include the following:

1. Computer skills
2. Good communication skills
3. Research abilities
4. Report writing
5. Time management
6. Organizational skills
7. Good work habits
8. Ability to work in a team
9. Customer service

Jeff was a client who had recently graduated with a B.S. in Business. We analyzed his work experience from his summer jobs at McDonald's and a warehouse, then wrote a great cover letter that got an interview with NYNEX.

Here's Jeff's Power Impact Technique letter:

Jeff Hillmere

72 Cleveland Circle
Brigton, MA 02131
(617) 555-0111

November 13, 1996

Bob Sewell, Product Manager
NYNEX
2223-112th Ave. NE
Boston, MA 02136

Re: Marketing/Customer Service Representative Position

Dear Mr. Sewell:

A motivated worker with a strong foundation in business and customer service is the background that I'd bring to your organization. I'm goal oriented, able to focus on the task with proven reliability to get the job done.

My strong interpersonal skills with extensive experience in building relationships and mediating problems or issues to find acceptable solutions has always been an asset to former employers. My computer skills are advanced and I excel at writing clear understandable reports or letters. I have logged hundreds of hours researching computerized databases. I am both quick and accurate on computerized entries.

I have well developed organizational and time management skills. I work well on my own, but always contribute to the team as a whole. I have developed work habits that will make me successful—attention to detail, pride in doing good work, excellent telephone and interpersonal skills, plus good conflict resolution abilities.

I would like to meet with you to discuss the valuable contributions I could make to your company. I can be reached at (617) 555-0111.

Your consideration and time is most appreciated.

Sincerely,

Jeff Hillmere

Jeff Hillmere

> *Jeff landed his first job, then excelled at NYNEX and received a promotion after his first year.*

The MBA Challenge

At one time an MBA was a ticket to some of the best jobs in the country. Today it is simply a part of the package of skills you sell to an employer.

One HR manager sent along this letter that she received from an MBA who sought a job within her organization. "Here's a classic," she wrote, "I can't believe anyone would send this out. It had a weak resumé and eleven—*eleven*—references listed. *Please!* This cover letter is so typical of what we get from these applicants. The 'I can do anything, but I don't know what position you would hire me for' type. You might want to show this as what *not* to do."

For confidentiality's sake, the name of the company and college have been changed to those of equal stature, but nothing else in this letter has been changed. Once you've read this letter, you will have a better understanding of why this company regards letters like these as truly wasted efforts.

One thing you should also realize is that Allen, our MBA letter writer, possesses some very important, usable skills that a company would find quite appealing if he would target his efforts toward specific jobs instead of using the poor approach shown here.

BAD COVER LETTER EXAMPLE

Allen Delloitson   777 Union Street #B2, Tallahassee, FL 32306 (904) 555-1111

Dear *United Parcel Service:*

As an MBA August of 1997 graduate student from Florida State University, I have taken an initiative to achieve and succeed at enterprising goals set before myself. Because I am a returning student, only adds to the fact that success is an important factor towards accomplishing these objectives. The *Presidents Honor Roll* (for three semesters), active participation in government issues (Hall Treasurer), and as a *volunteer manager* of KXRH radio station, along with examining and analyzing real businesses in Marketing, Management, and Finance projects, are all part of my formal education at Florida State.

A degree in Business Administration (Management) as of December 1995 and continued education into Florida State's *MBA* program (*Marketing/Finance*) in which I completed August of 1997 supports my ideology for success. Most companies are facing an ever increasing dilemma to cut cost, while maintaining a high quality product within a competitive environment. Teamwork and business backgrounds are essential for these requirements to be met. Recent cutbacks throughout most organizations and an increasingly competitive business environment support concern for this idea. Identifying specific functions that relate with each other to reduce redundancy and ultimately cut cost are going to be increasingly difficult. An adequate background in ACCOUNTING, MANAGEMENT, FINANCE, & MARKETING are essential tools for maintaining *United Parcel Service's* integrity, quality, and of course utilizing the organization's resources efficiently. Florida State's MBA program and my creative abilities meet these standards.

Team building, facilitating team interaction, coordinating, along with strategic planning are necessary tools I have acquired to accomplish the aforementioned tasks. Prior work experience (7 years prior to completion of degrees), ranging from some *management, sales, telemarketing, manufacturing and assembly* in addition to my formal education, have all contributed to my knowledge and understanding of organizations. These resources that I draw upon have taught invaluable lessons in teamwork, proper communication, strategic planning, leading, and creative thinking. Essential tools needed in any organization! These tools are necessary to build and facilitate competent teams within your organization and to *meet United Parcel Service's* goals.

My technical skills are vast compared to most business students. I have had training and experience in computer programming in HTML, Java, Basic and Pascal, along with using computers daily in work related fields. I am competent with Spreadsheets (Lotus, Excel), Word Processors (Word Perfect, Microsoft Word, Office Writer), Databases (Dbase IV, Access), Telecommunications (Pro Comm. Plus, TC) and Graphics and Presentation software (Harvard Graphics, Power Point). Consistent downloading from the Internet has taught me that new software takes little time to become acquainted with and master within short periods of time. Knowledge in Win95, Win 3.1, DOS, UNIX, OS/2 and using networks, along with IBM 3090E mainframe computers or the HP840 mini mainframe adds to further competence in computer literacy. Science courses along with reading about technology (because of interest in technology) and foreseeing future applications and directions of technology give me valuable insight to provide *United Parcel Service* with additional skills that the future will require.

My analytical and *communicative* abilities and background allow me interpret and then convey complicated areas of business, science, or technology into legible and comprehensible reasoning throughout the organization. As you know, this is an important factor by getting communicative goals conveyed without any misunderstanding of unclear issues, which can often be blown out proportion or misinterpreted. Because of this, I feel that *public relations* would be an additional area where my talents may help *United Parcel Service.* I have also demonstrated PR skills in previous work experience when addressing customers concerns and problems.

I hope that I have demonstrated sincere competence and the ability to meet the needs of your organization. I am hoping that *United Parcel Service* has a challenging, professional position for an ambitious MBA graduate with some prior work experience and who is willing to give a person of my talents and potential the chance to prove their worthiness. I would sincerely like to be a part of *United Parcel Service's* corporate team and the chance to contribute, in every way, to meet the needs of your organization through these changing times. My plans are simple, to be on the leading edge of technology, establish a loyalty to one company, facilitate teamwork, strategic planning, and accomplish organizational goals with integrity. I encourage you to consider me for the current *Compensation Analyst* position or any other Marketing, Finance, Human Resource, or Management positions within realm of *United Parcel Service's* organization.

Sincerely,

Allen Delloitson

ANALYSIS OF WHY THIS IS A POOR AND INEFFECTIVE COVER LETTER

✔ *Assumption that the MBA alone is so important* it will cause employers to read the letter. The reality is that numerous MBAs apply to major companies every week. A degree from a nonprestigious program is not a guaranteed door opener anymore.

✔ *The letter is too long, wordy, and has small type,* making it difficult to read.

✔ *Appears to be a form letter someone created,* and Allen has simply dropped in the employer's name as a mail-merged insert. The employer will suspect he mailed this to hundreds of companies nationwide, which I'm sure he did.

✔ *Lists job title in last line.* This appears to be an afterthought. He needed to quickly target one specific job at the top and simply outline the skills to do that job.

✔ *Too academic.* The writing seems too theory-based. The employer will quickly realize that this will be an employee who'll need *a lot* of training to become an asset.

✔ *First two paragraphs seem to sell the MBA program.* They do not underscore the skills he's learned or give evidence of any practical application, whether through specific projects or jobs he has held or a particular job he could perform.

✔ *Technical skills seem to be extensive, but he fails to draw any conclusions* regarding exactly the best ways to apply his skills in the job or the objectives he hopes to achieve.

✔ *Misused the term "public relations."* He clearly means customer service, not PR. (Specified PR skills are written promotion of the company or handling the media to gain positive publicity and exposure for the organization at the managerial level.)

✔ *Too many assumptions are made about the needs of the organization.* A lot of generalizations and preconceived notions are used to outline the company's needs, but they are not directed toward demonstrating how specific skills the candidate does possess can be used to perform a particular job.

✔ *Lists four different areas of interest* (marketing, finance, human resources, or management), but fails to offer any specific job titles—nor does he specifically target any one of those jobs with substance or summation of the key skills and strengths needed to do that job.

✔ *Focus is on Allen*—his goals, his dreams, his analysis of United Parcel Service—but he never takes it to the point of saying in a more clear and concise way: "This is what I can do for you . . ."

✔ *Poor closing statement.* "I'm hoping you have a challenging position for an ambitious MBA," he writes. Give me a chance. . . . To do what? That's certainly the question.

Allen would greatly benefit from using The Power Impact Technique to outline what the "compensation analyst" job is and how he meets the need. Certainly he could cite his computer and research skills plus any personnel course work that was related. The fact is, Allen is just so excited about getting his MBA that he may be in for a very enlightening experience when employers pitch this letter into the trash can along with the hundreds of others that come in just like it. *Moral of the story:*

✔ Use The Power Impact Technique to analyze the job and compose your letter.

✔ Apply for a specific job, detailing solid skills and practical application to do it.

✔ Keep potential and interest statements small but passionately focused on how the employer will benefit if you are hired.

✔ Apply for different positions by sending an entirely new cover letter with resumé and target it toward the job title you seek.

Career Changing

"I have hired people with very minimal experience simply because they 'sold me' on their talents and correlated what they had done with what the needs of my job required," said Margot Stanfield, vice president. She went on to offer this advice: "Sell me on what you can do. Sell me on 'why' you want the job, what you can do for me in this position, and then back it up with 'what' you've done in the past."

Changing careers can be a very frustrating and challenging process. It's difficult to find a good job and convince the employer to hire you. Most career changers have a more difficult time since they must decipher their own experience and skills, then translate those to meet an employer's needs. Leaving the military after 20 years of service and trying to move into the civilian world is certainly one of the hardest transitions to make. That's why I'm including Don's letter and experience of moving on after his career with the Navy ended.

One employer wrote us to say: "We got a lot of ex–military people applying for God-knows-what job. We almost always toss these since they rarely have jobs or past experience relative to us, nor do they ever outline any experience to show they can perform the job in question. They tend to include resumés that are very long, with huge lists of military things they've done. I feel sorry for these people; it's a tough transition to make, but all they want is a job, *any job,* and that's not what we hire for."

This employer makes an excellent point. Military people do need to research job duties for positions in the civilian market. A thorough analysis of jobs and tasks will better help you extract from your background only the information that is relevant to the job you are applying for. Then make your points on how you have performed and will perform the advertised tasks. That is indeed the only way to get an employer's interest.

Don was an engineer who'd spent most of his tours with the Navy on submarines. He spent three of his last five years working at the shipyard overseeing a major renovation project. We pulled out that experience, then emphasized his planning, organizational, and technical skills. Here's the letter he sent:

Donald Anderson
5011 N. Church Street
Norfolk, VA 23510
(757) 555-0111

May 4, 1997

Ms. Rita Cottrell
ABACUS Consultants, P.S.
One Center Avenue, South #201
Norfolk, VA 23512

Dear Ms. Cottrell:

Industrial Engineering Project Management, with experience in technical program development and coordination, consulting, liaison, field inspections, and construction management, is the expertise that I would bring to your Engineering Staff at ABACUS Consultants.

Aspects of my work experience that relate include providing engineering consulting to engineers and managers between the US Navy, Norfolk Naval Shipyard and Westinghouse. I've analyzed and solved power plant system problems. As the supervising Field Project Engineer, I monitored and evaluated the planning, scheduling and performance of system modifications and tests, and coordinated the development of new programs to improve efficiency. I have engineering design, plant operations, construction management, organizational leadership experience.

Additionally, I facilitated the efforts of approximately fifty, Department of Energy and shipyard, engineers and managers in developing cost-effective ways to inactivate nuclear submarines. I personally introduced several approaches that will save nearly $500,000 per submarine, and facilitated the efforts of this diverse group of experts towards even greater saving.

I have extensive computer skills which enabled me to develop a sophisticated database management system for our various shipyard projects. I feel my engineering project management, problem-solving, interpersonal and computer skills are assets I would bring to your Engineering Staff. I would like to meet with you to discuss how my experience would bring great added value to your organization. I can be reached at (757) 555-0111.

Your time and consideration are most appreciated.

Sincerely,

Donald Anderson

Donald Anderson

Special Notice for Those in the Creative Arts

Employers expect more creativity from those who make their living in desktop publishing, photography, or the graphic arts. Designs that scream loud graphics or are too faddy or trendy are not desired by our hiring managers. Innovation, with originality in the design, did set graphic artists, advertising, and publication specialists apart. Bob Christiano, owner of the Christiano Design Group and former creative director at a large advertising agency, offered these insights based on his years of hiring in this field: "I want to see something that's very creative but not trendy or out of a source book. I like something professional and unique or else just a plain letter. Anything in between shows lack of ambition that will surely be displayed on the job if I hire the person. Definitely forget that designer paper you buy in the office supply stores. You can't be unique when you are buying a mass-produced product everyone else has."

Too many graphic designs backfire. In this example, the client was unique in her design. It appeared on slate gray paper with complementing textured envelope. It has a simple but still contemporary design. It caught the manager's eye.

Anne got an immediate interview.

Anne Kim

July 8, 1997

Hilary Hyde
BUREAU OF EDUCATION AND RESEARCH
P O Box 96068
Washington, D.C. 20076

Dear Hilary,

As a highly productive desktop publisher who is always on-time and never misses a deadline, I would like to be considered for your Desktop Publishing position.

I bring extensive IBM and Macintosh experience; I can import and export documents with ease. I am proficient in Pagemaker, and Excel, and have several work samples I can show you that demonstrate the caliber of my work, including: charts, graphs, brochures, flyers and even a textbook. I received continuous praise for my creative designs while remaining within budget for both my current employer and freelance clients.

I would like the opportunity to show you my portfolio and discuss the valuable contributions I could bring to the Bureau. I can be reached at (202) 555-1212 to arrange a meeting.

Your time and consideration are most appreciated.

Sincerely,

Anne Kim

Anne Kim

More Examples of The Power Impact Technique at Work

Eileen is now this company's top salesperson!

Eileen Dyckman
933 Palm Court Drive
Santa Clara, CA 95054
(408) 555-0111

September 30, 1996

Mr. Henry Garrison
Continuex Corporation
One Plaza Square, Suite 1204
San Jose, CA 95050

Dear Mr. Garrison:

Fifteen years in computer systems management dealing with accounting, records and office management with ten years as top salesperson is the background I bring to your Software Sales position.

I have assisted over seventy-five offices in the conversion from manual to automated systems. I have generated increased profits by consistently selling add-ons such as training, technical support, customized applications and consulting services.

My experience in selling to vertical markets includes generating numerous referrals that I then am able to convert into sales.

I would like to meet with you to discuss the valuable contribution I might make to Continuex. I can be reached at (408) 555-0111.

Sincerely,

Eileen Dyckman

Eileen Dyckman

Enclosure

Anne Thompson
610 Center Street
Columbus, OH 43215
(614) 555-0111

December 3, 1996

Search Committee
Boys and Girls Club
17 Stone Street #111
Columbus, OH 43215

Dear Search Committee:

Twelve years experience in all aspects of development with a proven track record for building strong donor relationships, significantly improving giving programs, organizing profitable events and implementing successful direct mail programs is the background I'd bring to your Development Director position. Highlights of my previous accomplishments include:

- Implemented an emergency fundraising plan when nonprofit lost $450,000 of its funding. In one year raised $750,000.
- Implemented direct mail programs, raised $200,000.
- Established new major gifts campaign. Recruited and trained 80 high profile volunteers, $450,000+ raised.
- Planned and coordinated hundreds of special events: dinners, galas, receptions, luncheons, auctions, phonathons, educational programs, and conferences.
- Recruited, selected, and trained 400+ volunteers obtaining high levels of work effort, commitment, and financial support.
- Negotiated 100+ vendor contracts including hotels, catering, prizes. Obtained better terms, lower costs, and promotional tie-ins.
- Featured in on-air interviews for WIRO-TV and WTSS-TV.

I would like to meet with you to discuss the important contributions I could make to the Boys and Girls Club. I can be reached at (614) 555-0111. Your time and consideration are most appreciated.

Sincerely,

Anne Thompson

Anne Thompson

Patricia O'Keefe

200 East 30th Apt. 12B
New York, NY 10017
(212) 555-0111

September 7, 1997

School of Medicine SC-64
Columbia University
New York, NY 10027

Dear Dr. Bjurstrom:

With extensive experience in managed care administration, strategic planning and physician, executive and clinical recruitment, I would bring a unique set of skills to the position, Director of Clinical Services and Networks.

Highlights of my relevant experience include:

- Team member to establish a statewide HMO owned by the Catholic Medical Center.
- Responsible for developing provider network of 400 plus physicians in New York City and Philadelphia.
- Fifteen years involvement in developing hospital networks and strategic plans.
- Consultant to over 45 physician groups and hospitals assessing their practice opportunities, advising them on practice structure and compensation, and then recruiting the needed physicians.
- Team member conducting budget and strategic plan audits on 32 hospitals.

Dr. Bjurstrom, we met briefly a few years ago when you were at Multicare and I was doing a search for a Neurosurgeon to join the Mt. Sinai medical staff. Although the search was aborted, your name was mentioned by Mary Smith, President of MD Resources, when she would see you at ACPE meetings. She has decided to close the Eastcoast office of MD Resources. Thus, since New York is my home, I am beginning a job search. The position you are offering sounds very exciting to me, an opportunity to work with physicians in an academic setting and to make a contribution to the inevitable changes academic medicine must go through as all of healthcare delivery and financing reorganizes.

I would like to get together with you for a brief meeting and discuss my contribution to your network. I can be reached at (212) 555-0111. I look forward to meeting with you again soon.

Sincerely,

Patricia O'Keefe

Patricia O'Keefe

Pat got the interview over 300 others!

Brian Martins
667 Charlestown Blvd.
Las Vegas, NV 89109
(702) 555-0111

August 23, 1997

Jay Construction Company
1164 Thomas Street
Las Vegas, NV 89105
RE: Project Management Position

Dear Jay Construction Company:

Twenty years in the construction industry with the last eight in large scale commercial project management summarizes the background I'd bring to your Project Manager position. I possess proven expertise in developing *accurate* bids, contract negotiations, streamlining costs, and bringing projects in on time and within budget.

Highlights of my recent background include:

- Establish computerized job costing system for accurate job cost analysis.
- Management of seven projects up to $8 million.
- Streamlined management costs saving $100,000 annually.
- Brought $1.4M project in $120,000 *under* budget. Additional shared profit of $48,000.

I am immediately available to begin making contributions to your company. I can be reached at (702) 555-0111 to arrange a meeting.

Sincerely,

Brian Martins

Brian Martins

Brian landed the job and a higher salary than before he was laid off. Being over 50 proved not to be a problem.

Colleen loves this new job!

Colleen Riggins
3 Strayer St.
Oklahoma City, OK 73159
(405) 555-0111

January 17, 1997

Mr. Buspy
Chemicals Inc.
1233 Regal Row
Oklahoma City, OK 73154

Dear Mr. Buspy:

In the last 10 years while I served as an executive assistant, I have developed the skills that ensure the highest level of competence, time management, confidentiality and a sincere desire to make my boss' job easier.

As your assistant you can expect the same skills that past employers have praised:

- Loyalty and service.
- Competence with intricate attention to details.
- Customer service and problem solving abilities.
- Proficient computer and office skills.
- Time management in high pressure situations.
- Extensive meeting planning experience.

Most importantly, I quickly learn your preferences, your objectives and your goals and do my very best to aid you in the leadership of the company. I do hope we can meet for a short time so I could explain more fully the valuable contributions I could make as your executive assistant. I can be reached at (405) 555-0111.

Your time and consideration are most appreciated.

Sincerely,

Colleen Riggins

Colleen Riggins

Mark Shaw
167 Sunset Blvd. #313
Los Angeles, CA 90067
(213) 555-0111

March 2, 1996

Jack Sanborn
WNBC TV
1 Disney Street
Los Angeles, CA 90061

Dear Jack:

16 years of broadcast engineering experience, in both radio and television with the most recent as chief engineer of WABC-TV, providing the highest quality on-air reliability briefly summarizes my background.

My experience includes:

- Perfect FCC compliance, never receiving a citation (saving the stations anywhere from $5,000–$80,000 in fines).
- Recognition as a leading expert in the local engineering broadcast area, continuously informed on the latest technological innovations, advancements, and equipment development.
- Years of troubleshooting technical problems including numerous complicated remote transmissions.
- Installation of 5 new transmitters.
- Budget management over $300,000.

I pride myself in making my stations on-air sound and look better than the competition's. My approach is to give 150% to any job I undertake. My success as a manager has been founded, not only in my excellent technical abilities, but also in the skills I utilize to work effectively with operators and talent.

I would like to arrange a brief meeting to discuss in detail the valuable contributions I can bring to WNBC. I can be reached at (213) 555-0111.

Your time and consideration are most appreciated.

Sincerely,

Mark Shaw

Mark Shaw

Danielle Whitfield
42 Barker St.
Jamesville, NY 13121
(315) 555-0111

May 23, 1997

Sharon Wright
Medical Affairs
News and Community Relations
University Medical Center, SC-60
Syracuse, NY 13109

Dear Ms. Wright:

Promoting the University Medical Center can be competitive during this era of healthcare reform, when so many providers are vying for positive visibility and recognition in the media. Your Media Specialist must have a good understanding of the needs and interests of the news media, be a seasoned public relations professional who is adept at capturing the attention of the media, and have a strong professional background working within the health care industry.

My background is a good match with your needs as I bring five professional years of PR experience. Highlights of my experience include:

- Effectively pitching stories to news media resulting in published articles in both local and national newspapers.
- Researching and writing dozens of articles for magazines and newsletters.
- Interviewing numerous individuals to gather facts, details and personal stories to create appropriate reports, articles, news hooks and marketing benefits.
- Utilizing many desktop publishing programs to create brochures, newsletters, flyers and articles.

I believe I could make a strong contribution to your efforts in maintaining strong news media and community relations. I can be reached at (315) 555-0111 to discuss this in further detail. Your consideration is most appreciated.

Sincerely,

Danielle Whitfield

Danielle Whitfield

> *Danielle landed the interview, beating out nearly 400 others!*

Salary History Requests

Money—We all care about it! Most would certainly like to have more of it. *Money.* And oh, how those salary questions are designed to eliminate job hunters from the pack. Employers place those salary questions in their ads to trick you. According to our survey, 23% of the employers do request salary information in their ads. Martha Steinborn, an HR consultant for employers who's hired hundreds of people in her career, says she always advises her clients (employers) to request a salary history. The reasons to do so are to screen out those who are too high or too low and to determine an average salary that people are paid for similar jobs in other places. Additionally, she noted, "Previous salary tells something about what they were really doing in past jobs." Wow—there's an insight for you! The bottom line is that salary info is used to *eliminate* you. I recommend that when you see the phrase "send salary history," you simply don't do it. Focus on skills and use The Power Impact Technique. If you're like many of my clients, you'll get called in for an interview without ever providing that financial background.

One word of caution, though. A human resource director from a major bank told us about a mistake that people tend to make in addressing the salary issue. "People tend to 'inflate' their current salary," she noted. Since an employer could then check on this figure, it's best never to offer exactly what you are or were making. There is more leeway to negotiate higher compensation when your future employer doesn't know exactly what you made before. There are *some* employers out there, though, who are adamant in learning what your salary requirements are. Their ads typically state: "Send salary history, without which you won't be considered for the position."

Knowing you want to eventually negotiate the highest salary possible, my advice is to just quote a salary survey source and claim to be within that range. It has worked for hundreds of clients, and this technique allowed Paula to obtain a salary $6,000 higher than she had earned with her previous employer, whom she wanted to leave for underpaying her.

Here's her Power Impact Technique letter. Note that the salary info is near the bottom, after all her important skills and contributions have been stressed.

Paula Lazetti
72 Court Street #21B
Queens, New York 10066
(212) 555-0111

November 15, 1996

Ms. Monica Pierce, CFO
Pacific Import Corporation
5930-5th Avenue, Suite 700
New York, NY 10060

Dear Ms. Pierce:

Ten years of experience in collections and credit, with more than six years at a managerial level, plus proven expertise in collecting funds while building and maintaining positive relationships with customers and staff, are just part of the knowledge I would bring to your position of Credit and Collections Manager. In addition to these qualifications, I possess the following abilities and beliefs:

- Establishment of policies and procedures to improve and maintain a consistent cash flow that ensures the company's stability and profitability.
- A philosophy that it is the credit department's responsibility to assist with increasing sales while minimizing the risk of bad debt loss.
- Experience with area collection agencies, attorneys, small claims courts and providers of credit reports, and the ability to know when to use which service.
- Supervisory experience that includes screening resumés, interviewing, training, utilizing employee strengths and encouraging their professional development.
- Continually working on increasing my knowledge and education to keep apprised of the latest trends in the ever changing world of credit and business.

At your request, my salary expectations are based on the national credit association's annual survey. Credit managers of mid-size companies average $32,000–$45,000 and I'm within that range with benefits and bonuses being an additional part of the compensation package.

Enclosed is my resumé for your consideration. I would be very interested in discussing this position with you further, and can be reached at (212) 555-0111. I look forward to discussing how I can become a valuable asset and contributor for your organization.

Sincerely,

Paula Lazetti

Paula Lazetti

Summary

Hiring managers selected The Power Impact Technique as their preferred style to write a cover letter. Many stated that it concisely and quickly tells them the specific skills you can offer to fit their needs. Richard, a vice president of human resources for a major manufacturer advises, "Get to the point—fast. Tell me your background and how it applies to my company. Point out any success relevant to my needs. That's the kind of letter I want to read." Focusing on the employers' needs is the key to getting hired. Our conclusion: Use The Power Impact Technique. It works!

WRITING YOUR COVER LETTERS

The Writing Technique

Let's use The Power Impact Technique to write an easy and highly influential cover letter for you. To begin we must analyze the job you are applying for. In our example here, we've italicized the important points for the letter's emphasis:

JOB ANALYSIS

TEACHER

Pinehurst Elementary School seeks *experienced Second Grade Teacher*. Must possess *Valid Florida State Teacher's License*. Experience using *Whole Language Reading Programs* preferred. The District is an equal opportunity employer. Minorities are encouraged to apply. Send resumé and three letters of reference to:

Second Grade Search Committee
Orlando Public Schools
Superintendent's Office
1 Disney Drive
Orlando, FL 32809

Employer's NOTED NEEDS:

1. Valid teacher's license

2. Whole language reading program experience

3. Experienced teacher

ASSUMED NEEDS: These are attributes necessary to perform the job that are not specifically mentioned, but you know from your previous job that they are important.

1. Creating lesson plans
2. Committee work

Now it's your turn to analyze the particular want ad or job description you wish to apply for and fill in both the NOTED and ASSUMED NEEDS.

Employer's NOTED NEEDS:

1. _____

2. _____

3. _____

4. _____

5. _____

Employer's ASSUMED NEEDS:

1. _____

2. _____

3. _____

4. _____

5. _____

Our next step is to link the employer's need with your skill(s):

Employer's need: Experienced and licensed teacher

Her skills: Three years elementary teaching with valid license in Florida

Now it's your turn. List all that are mentioned:

1. Employer's NOTED NEED:

_____

_____

Your skill to meet that need:

_____

_____

_____

_____

2. Employer's NOTED NEED:

_____

_____

Your skill to meet that need:

_____

_____

_____

_____

3. Employer's NOTED NEED:

_____

_____

Your skill to meet that need:

_____

_____

_____

_____

Now write down what you believe to be important assumed needs:

1. Employer's ASSUMED NEED:

_____

_____

Your skill to meet that need:

_____

_____

_____

_____

_____

2. Employer's ASSUMED NEED:

_____

_____

Your skill to meet that need:

_____

_____

_____

_____

_____

Note anything of personal relevance to substantiate why you'd be interested in this job, organization, or company:

_____

_____

Next, list the top skills you have to sell based on your analysis of the job. Experience is always a good place to start. Review the important skills the employer requires and what you've written down. Outline below the important points to mention in the opening.

Your *top* skills to mention in opening paragraph:

_____

_____

_____

_____

For example, our teacher wrote:

1. Three years as a second grade teacher
2. Created hundreds of lesson plans
3. Member of team that developed a new reading program for entire district

Next, we need to create the first high-impact sentence. Our teacher wrote:

> Three years as a Florida public school second grade teacher with experience introducing the Whole Language Reading Curriculum into the District is the background I'd bring to your Second Grade Teaching Position.

Note: Always identify the job you are applying for. In this candidate's case, it was for a "Second Grade Teacher" position. Also, we felt it was important to balance her few years' experience with the necessary reading program experience.

Create your opening sentence:

_____

_____

_____

_____

Now insert your skills that address both their NOTED and ASSUMED NEEDS:

_____

_____

_____

_____

Our teacher wrote:

I find it immensely satisfying to come to work each day and greet my eager class. I work hard to encourage learning with creativity that makes it a fun process. I've developed hundreds of lesson plans that utilize history, current events, art, and music to achieve the learning objectives of my diverse-needs class. Two years ago, I was a team member who reviewed numerous reading curriculum. The Whole Language Reading System was selected. Last year, I introduced that reading program in a beta test project to my class. We had excellent results, and the entire district has now adopted the program.

Our teacher felt it was important to include why she was available and to offer a recommendation to the employer. She did this also to personalize her letter. Although in most cases it is not wise to add too much personal information, it made sense here. Her husband's new employer—Disney—was a stable company that would not likely require them to move again soon. She wrote:

I sadly left Viewmont behind, as my husband's new job with Disney has permanently relocated us to Orlando. I encourage you to contact my principal, Mrs. Smith, to learn firsthand about the valuable contributions I made while at Viewmont and the success I had with the Whole Language Reading System.

I would like to discuss in greater detail your current needs and how I might be an asset to your school. I can be reached at (407) 555-1212.

Your time and thoughtful consideration are appreciated.

Sincerely,
Second Grade Teacher (who really wants the job)

Add anything that will personalize your letter:

_____

_____

_____

_____

_____

Here's our second grade teacher's entire Power Impact Technique™ letter:

Wendy Teacher
I Mickey Mouse Street
Orlando, FL 32812
(407) 555-1212

Dear Principal,

Three years as a Florida public school second grade teacher with experience introducing the Whole Language Reading Curriculum into the District is the background I'd bring to your Second Grade Teaching Position. I find it immensely satisfying to come to work each day and greet my eager class. I work hard to encourage learning with creativity that makes it a fun process. I've developed hundreds of lesson plans that utilize history, current events, art, and music to achieve the learning objectives of my diverse-needs class.

Two years ago, I was a team member who reviewed numerous reading curriculum, the Whole Reading Curriculum and the Whole Language System was selected. Last year, I introduced that reading program in a beta test project to my class. We had excellent results, and the entire district has now adopted the program.

I sadly left Viewmont behind, as my husband's new job has permanently relocated us to Orlando. I encourage you to contact my principal, Mrs. Smith, to learn firsthand about the valuable contributions I made while at Viewmont and the success I had with the Whole Language Reading System. I would like to discuss in greater detail your current needs and how I might be an asset to your school. I can be reached at (407) 555-1212.

Your time and thoughtful consideration are appreciated.

Sincerely,

Wendy Teacher

Wendy Teacher

Or, we could use the bulleted list approach. One style may be easier for you to use. Our teacher selected the paragraph style, but the bulleted list style would have worked for her, too. Here's what the bulleted style would have looked like:

**Wendy did land
this job!**

Wendy Teacher
1 Mickey Mouse Street
Orlando, FL 32812
(407) 555-1212

Dear Principal,

Three years as a Florida public school second grade teacher with experience introducing the Whole Language Reading Curriculum into the District is the background I'd bring to your Second Grade Teaching Position.

Highlights of my background include:

- Possess valid elementary teacher's certificate.
- Committee member on evaluating and selecting new district reading program.
- Adapted and introduced "Whole Language Reading Program" in second grade classroom with excellent results.
- Experience handling children with diverse cultural and educational needs.
- Created hundreds of lesson plans utilizing proven educational materials with creativity that makes learning enjoyable for the students.

My husband's new job has permanently relocated us to Orlando. I encourage you to contact my principal, Mrs. Smith, to learn firsthand about the valuable contributions I made while at Viewmont and the success I had with the Whole Language Reading System. I would like to discuss in greater detail your current needs and how I might be an asset to your school. I can be reached at (407) 555-1212.

Your time and thoughtful consideration are appreciated.

Sincerely,

Wendy Teacher

Wendy Teacher

Now you can clearly see exactly how this works: the strong opening, a powerful body with evidence she can do the job, even an explanation about her desire to move to a new school.

Back to *you* and finishing *your* letter. We're almost done. Now it's time to end your own letter. David, a senior human resources director for one of Boston's top companies, warns us about making unsubstantiated claims. He advises job hunters to avoid using pat phrases such as, "I know I can help your company reach its goals." It is more effective to follow through with the emphasis that you are a person who is focused on filling the employer's needs.

This closing is both positive and strong:

> I'd like to discuss in greater detail the value contributions I would make to your *the company name*. I can be reached at *your phone number*. Your time and consideration are appreciated.
>
> Sincerely,
>
> *Your Name*
>
> Your Name

Now your letter is complete. Wasn't that a lot easier than you thought it would be? Once you use The Power Impact Technique, you'll have such great success that you'll never write a cover letter any other way. These letters will save you a lot of time and wasted efforts. Be sure to keep a copy of every letter you write (see Chapter 8). Most can be adapted with a little finessing, and then they'll be ready to send out at the next opportunity.

CAREER COACH *tip*

Power Impact Technique letters get employers' attention!

Paper, Printing, and Envelope Recommendations

Our 600 employers surveyed stated definite preferences on how letters should appear. I base my following recommendations on those survey results:

Paper:	Matches resumé; rich texture, laid, or woven.
Letterhead:	Create a simple letterhead with centered name, address, and phone number (e-mail is optional).
Color:	White, off-white, or ivory.
Borders, colors:	*Not* impressive. Several noted a negative impact. (Exceptions are graphic artists, photographers, and artists.)
Format:	Easy-to-read, one-page format looks best.
Envelopes:	Standard business size. Typed (or laser-printed) address preferred. (Good penmanship is acceptable, but less recommended.)
Designer paper:	84% of employers found fancy designer paper not influential. 16% were positively influential. Recommendation is to write a well-formatted letter on plain paper with a rich texture. No designs.
Return address:	Typed or laser-printed. No cutesy address label designs.
Printing:	Laser-printed, for crisp, sharp copy.

SPECIAL LETTERS THAT CRACK THE HIDDEN JOB MARKET

6

According to the Department of Labor, 85% of all jobs are never advertised. One of the very best ways to discover these terrific opportunities is to send letters targeted to hiring managers. Notice I did *not* say to personnel. Mailing out 100 resumés with a generic cover letter blanketing every personnel office in your region is a complete waste of time and money. Personnel's job is to screen people *out* of consideration, not to hire you.

In today's competitive job market, you must be more savvy than ever before. Self-marketing letters should be a vital part of your job search efforts. There are two types of self-marketing letters I've found that work exceedingly well. The first approach I recommend is a letter advertising your skills and inquiring about openings, called the Prospect Letter. The second is a request for some guidance on your job hunting activities—a technique that's called *Informational Interviewing*. Both tap into the hidden job market and can produce some pretty terrific leads if you follow the formula I've outlined. The idea behind this strategy is to uncover potential openings. Acknowledge that you aren't aware of what the employer's current needs are. Many times, personnel or most of the other employees do not know *all* the jobs that are open or *may become available* in the near future. You learn firsthand, from the person who would likely be your boss, exactly what the hiring situation is. The nicest thing about this technique is that it allows you to be proactive. You sit in the driver's seat and take control of your job search. You make up the list of potential companies that appeal to you based on their reputation, corporate culture, product, or service. This allows you to align your interests and match them with potential employers who might be able to use your

85% of all jobs are not advertised. These self-marketing letters open the door to an abundance of great jobs with the better employers.

skills. This is the best way to uncover terrific jobs with companies where you are likely to find satisfying work. Follow the guidelines for both techniques—they can yield some good results as they provide the opportunity to learn exactly what an employer needs or wants.

Prospect Letters

There are five important tips to making the Prospect Letters produce interest and results. They are:

Tip #1: Develop a list of companies you want to work for.   Examine your interests and narrow your targets to pick out the corporate culture that seems to be a match for you and your work style. The library is the best place to develop this list. Check out reference manuals, old newspapers, magazines, business directories, and annual reports. *Infotrac,* a computerized service listing magazine and newspaper articles that have been published during the last three years, is a good resource. Browse through professional association directories and make note of *where* people work. Competitors of your current employer or industry leaders might be other organizations you'll want to add to your list. You need to create a list of no less than 30 potential employers.

Tip #2: Have a clearly defined job target.   "Any job" won't work. When using this technique, you must be specific. You need to succinctly summarize some important skills to arouse the employer's interest. You may have different jobs you want to target. That's okay, but do keep good records of what was sent where. When considering a large company, you may need to approach various managers who supervise the area of interest. I do not recommend that you mail out different job targets *at the same time to the same employer.* Better to start with one specific position and learn of its potential, then move on to another department in that company with a different supervisor if your current job target is not available.

Tip #3: Identify the person most likely to hire for the position you desire. You must write to your potential boss. Call the department and ask for the name of the person in charge of the department. Spell the name correctly, get the complete, accurate mailing address, and note the phone number. This may take a little or a great deal of research time, depending on the employer. For example, at large companies like Motorola with over 100,000 employees or Pepsi with over 370,000 workers, it may take some significant effort to identify the potential manager (or managers) to write to. Ask your friends, family, and even college alumni to help. *Network.* Depending on the type of job you seek, you might find that there are several managers you could potentially go to work for. Detective skills are necessary. You'll need to uncover names and phone numbers. Later, you will follow up and learn exactly what the true hiring picture looks like for that organization.

Tip #4: Write an enticing self-marketing letter.   Samples follow on the next few pages. Be sure to send along your resumé. Your letter must specifically target the job you want to do. It's a few teasing sentences that will catch the manager's eye. Keep it short and to the point.

Tip #5: Follow up and call the employer.   Within 7 to 10 days after mailing, make the follow-up phone call, which is both important and necessary. Your letter gives you a great reason to talk to the employer about his or her hiring needs. It's a good idea to write out an actual script of what you'll say to the employer. Start out by encapsulating your background: "I've got 10 years in magazine advertising sales for a monthly edition and sent you a letter last week. Have you seen it yet?"

This opening is to pique interest. There are only two answers—yes or no. If the employer says yes or is vaguely trying to recall your letter, just jump into a short spiel on your background. Ask about upcoming openings or current needs. If there are no jobs available, conclude with this question: "Do you know of anyone seeking a sales rep [*fill in the title you're seeking*] with my background?" This allows the employer to pass on any job leads he or she may have heard of. These letters have been highly effective in securing interviews for my clients, and they often lead to landing very good jobs.

If you are not employed, plan to mail at least two or three letters every week. If you have a job, you have less time available. Mailing just one letter per week and following up is manageable. After 10 weeks, you'll hit 10 employers. Soon you'll be swimming in numerous employment opportunities.

Prospect Letter

Barry Laird

1 Main Street
City, NY 11111
(212) 555-0111

August 5, 1997

Dear Evelyn:

Mike Thomas, who is familiar with my background in the pulp and paper industry managing companies through growth and change to lead them to profitability, suggested I contact you to learn more about Simpson's management needs.

My strengths lie in leading companies through re-engineering and expansion. I build strong teams that achieved high levels of productivity. I have a proven track record as General Manager for Midgard, in which we reduced labor costs and increased sales. Our profits advanced 11% while I was there.

Mike felt that we may have a common need—I wish to remain in the region and use my abilities to enhance a company to new levels of profitability, and you may be seeking new leadership.

I'll call you next week to arrange a meeting or you can reach me at (212) 555-0111.

Your time and consideration are appreciated.

Sincerely,

Barry Laird

Barry Laird

Enclosure: Resumé

> **This employer had no position but gave Barry two leads for employers who did have openings.**

Prospect Letter

Ed Rowoth
1 Main Street
City, NY 11111
(201) 555-0111

June 15, 1997

MIS Director
Med-Life Systems
PO Box 12002
Maple Grove, Minnesota 55343

Dear MIS Director:

With proven expertise in business and information systems, I would bring excellent experience increasing productivity while containing costs to your MIS team.

Some highlights of my background include:

- 5 years managing information systems on Mainframe, Mini, UNIX and PC Networks within a manufacturing environment.
- Fluent in C, FORTRAN, COBOL, and PASCAL programming languages.
- Both conversion and system upgrade experience.
- Established complete work flow re-engineering process that resulted in 20% increase in productivity.

I would like to discuss in greater detail the valuable contributions I would bring to your MIS team. I'll contact you in a few days as to what your current and future needs might be.

Your time and consideration is appreciated.

Sincerely,

Ed Rowoth

Ed Rowoth

Enclosure: Resumé

Prospect Letter

Sandra Harrington
1 Main Street
City, NY 11111
(212) 555-0111

September 16, 1997

Mr. John Thomas, Vice President
Apple South Inc.
One Washington Avenue
Madison, GA 30650

Dear Mr. Thomas:

Are you currently looking for an Executive Assistant who is recognized for having outstanding organizational skills with high levels of productivity? An employee who has a track record of efficiency in producing a finished work product with no mistakes? Are you interested in a highly organized assistant that continually saves you time?

Let me assure you that you can verify this information by speaking to any of my former employers. They will tell you that I bring the above skills to your company. Additionally, I have the following expertise:

- Advanced computer skills
- Meeting planning experience
- Managing operational budgets
- Human resource background
- Project management on multiple and difficult projects

I can be reached at (212) 555-0111 to discuss your current needs.

Thank you for your time and consideration.

Very truly yours,

Sandra Harrington

Sandra Harrington

This letter is how Sandra met her new boss.

Informational Interview Request

The second approach for self-marketing letters is designed to develop your network and gain more knowledge about companies, the field and potential job openings. The Informational Interview has been used by job hunters for over 15 years, but you can still obtain excellent results when this technique is properly executed. There are a couple drawbacks. many people have abused this technique by *requesting information* and then at the meeting asking if the employer has a job for them. This lie—for that's what it is—has angered and alienated many managers. Some may be quite leery about granting your request. This is most true in popular areas such as film, broadcasting, journalism and public relations, where getting jobs is tremendously challenging and highly competitive.

Next, this technique can be extremely time-consuming. Arranging meetings, dressing up, going to the informational interview, and returning can take several hours per session. Although the ideal situation is to have a face-to-face interview and get a firsthand look inside the employer's organization, this may not be an option. Face-to-face you do obtain a more solid impression of life inside the company. Many busy professionals, though, will be worried that you'll stay an hour instead of the 15 minutes you requested. Therefore, many of your informational interviews will be conducted by phone due to time constraints (yours or theirs).

The major reason to utilize Informational Interviews is to learn firsthand about the skills the employer values, plus you'll gain insights into the company, field, or career. You will get job leads.

Some job openings you are likely to be told about are wonderful fits for your abilities, experience, talents, and interests. Every one of these letters produced meetings for my clients and led to conversations with hiring managers. This letter technique was exactly how Sue met her future sales manager and Kevin got introduced to the controller who eventually hired him. You might be wondering, why write a letter at all? Why not just call the person and suggest the meeting? That is certainly the ideal and fastest way to do this. But—and this a big *but*—I find most people simply agonize over phoning strangers. Whenever I ask my seminar classes how many will just go and call the employer, only 10% of the people raise their hands. Nearly 90% won't. When given the option to *write first,* almost all would follow up, knowing that the employer is *expecting* the phone call. The important point is to get you to reach and talk to the employer. An added bonus the letter offers is that you get to place your resumé in the employer's hands before you visit to open up the possibilities more quickly.

The guidelines to request an Informational Interview are as follows:

Tip #1: Use a referral's name whenever possible. Ask family, friends, coworkers, colleagues, neighbors, and even college alumni to help you. Identify some good people to talk to who may share the names of someone in your type of job or inside a company you want to work for. "Name-drop," with a "Jack suggested that I call." A referral will make it easier for you to get people to be receptive, talkative, and more willing to help you out.

Tip #2: Send a resumé. This should accompany your letter. It allows the person to get an idea about your background and level of experience. It will help your contact to advise you more appropriately.

Tip #3: Limit your visit to 15 minutes. Most busy executives cannot afford to give you much more than that without having to work over-time. Since you are trying to create new, helpful friends, watch the clock—once 20 minutes has passed, ask to schedule another meeting in a couple weeks. This shows respect for your contact's time and generosity.

Tip #4: Be prepared. At the beginning of the interview, summarize your background with a brief introduction. Bring a list of written questions, asking the most important ones first. Take advantage of the opportunity to inquire about what skills the employer deems most important to suc-ceed at the job you desire. Also ask about future plans, products, or growth.

Tip #5: Go in with no expectations. Reassure the person you don't expect him or her to know about a job or have a job—you just need advice. Going into an interview expecting someone to get you a job can really sabotage your results. You must anticipate getting ideas or leads—nothing more.

Tip #6: Help them help you. Prepare a list of companies you're inter-ested in. Ask your contact to look at the list. Inquire if the person could suggest any *other* companies that you should add to your list to contact. Having a list ready is important, because your contact will be quickly scanning it. It will enable the manager to think of more companies (particularly small ones) that you are unlikely to know about. If you are conducting this interview over the phone, offer to e-mail your list, or simply mention six or seven other companies. Offering names will give the manager ideas, and you'll get more suggestions from this free-association technique.

Tip #7: Ask for a referral. Do they know anyone who works at the companies on your list? Stress that they can work in any department, as you are simply trying to get as much inside information as possible. Also inquire if they know of any other person in general who would be helpful in advising you on your job search. Tell them you plan to follow up on their recommendations soon.

Tip #8: Send a thank-you note. People's time and help are important. Tell them their advice was valuable in a short, handwritten note. You must do this for every person you meet. Always ask for a person's business card—it will make it easier for you to know exactly where to mail your note. As a matter of politeness, people will often say, "Keep me posted." But unless they are close friends, they rarely mean it. Form letters sent out months after this meeting announcing your new position are not necessary or wanted. Send a note to announce your success only if it'll be personalized and if the individual receiving it is being thanked and credited for assisting you in obtaining the job you accepted. During the job hunting process, phone your contacts six or eight weeks later to check on whether they have heard of any positions. Don't be bothersome, just friendly, and never push or beg them to help you. One HR manager noted: "I hate it when people beg—their desperation is a major turnoff." Professional inquiries will get you much further with the hiring personnel. Arrange one to three informational interviews per week. You'll make new friends, gain access to a lot of insider information, and get some very good job leads that will result in actual interviews and, potentially, a new position.

Informational Interview Request—
No Referral

Annette Spiegal
1 Main Street
City, NY 11111
(201) 555-0111

November 5, 1996

Dear Mary Tightwater,

I am writing to ask for your help and guidance. Community Home Healthcare has downsized dramatically and I now seek to employ my fundraising skills with a new organization where I will use my passion, enthusiasm, and determination to raise funds for their important cause.

Here's how you can help me. I'd like to set up a brief 15 minute (meeting or phone chat) to seek your advice on my job search. Let me assure you, I don't expect you to have a job or know about a job. I simply want your guidance. I have attached my resumé so you will be better able to direct me when we talk.

I appreciate your assistance in my search.

Thank you,

Annette Spiegal

Annette Spiegal

Annette got terrific leads and two job offers.

Informational Interview Request:
Special Angle—Relocation

Sue Frothsinger
1 Main Street
City, NY 11111
(201) 555-0111

June 15, 1997

Mr. Walter Fugiwara
Advertising Director
San Francisco Magazine
2520 Camino Diablo, Suite 200
Walnut Creek, CA 94596

Dear Mr. Fujiwara:

Fifteen years of success, working in Sales and Advertising for regional magazines and newspapers briefly encapsulates my background. As I have just relocated back to the Bay Area, I am writing to you to ask for guidance. Let me assure you, Jim, I do not expect you to have a job or even know about a job. In your position at San Francisco Magazine, you are in an excellent position to guide and advise me with my job search.

I would like to meet for just 15 minutes to gain your professional advice. I would be happy to share some of the innovative ideas we have recently introduced at Pacific Northwest and Seattle Magazines. I will contact you in a few days to arrange a meeting.

Your time and assistance is most appreciated.

Sincerely,

Sue Frothsinger

Sue Frothsinger

Informational Interview Request—
New Graduate Angle with Referral

Kevin Lash
1 Main Street
City, NY 11111
(201) 555-0111

July 8, 1996

Dear Ms. Stone,

Roy Bingham recommended I contact you as he felt you could be most helpful in providing me with some guidance.

I am a recent graduate from University of Ohio in Accounting and Finance. *USA Today* has quoted this as the worst job market in 10 years for new college grads. I do not believe this is true about a hardworking, eager person such as myself. Besides my good accounting foundation, I have strong computer skills including database creation, establishment of inventory tracking systems and have developed good client rapport building skills. This is the foundation I'd bring to an accounting or finance position. I also offer specific experience as Home Depot's Property Management intern, plus inventory tracking and customer services experience.

I don't expect you to know about a job, Ms. Stone, or have a job available. Roy thought if you'd just spend 15 minutes offering your expert guidance it would greatly help my job search.

I will call you next week to arrange a brief meeting.

Your time and assistance is greatly appreciated.

Sincerely,

Kevin Lash

Kevin Lash

Kevin found a great job using this approach.

Thank-You Letters

An important but often neglected part of the job search process is to send a thank-you letter after an interview. Sam's experience (in Chapter 3) is a good testimonial to show how important this step is. Hard-sell approaches (e.g., "Hire me") are not successful—so be sure to be more sincere in your approach. I have found handwritten notes to be quite effective, but you can type a letter if you prefer.

Several employers tell me that thank-you notes demonstrate true interest in the job. If the employer is on the fence between you and some-one else, you can tip the scale in your favor with a well-worded thank-you note. The examples that follow include a handwritten note card plus Ken's letter, both sent to stress these candidates' enthusiasm for the job. Additionally, they reiterated a couple of the top skills they would bring to the job. Kristen, on the other hand, had called me in a panic when her interview lasted only 20 minutes. Her company had gone through a merger and every employee had to reapply for their jobs. In Kristen's case, the position would be a promotion. She was competing against several highly qualified individuals for the project manager job. Knowing that only a few managers would be "rehired," and more than 100 would be laid off, she was very nervous about the shortness of the interview (though everyone's was about that length as it turned out). She said in an exasperated tone, "I was so nervous since I hadn't interviewed in 13 years and I know I did a lousy job. I don't think I told them what I could really do and have done. Should I call and explain about being nervous and all?" I told her no, but that writing a good thank-you letter would accomplish the goal in a highly professional way. So we put together her strongest skills and she faxed the letter to the interviewers that same day. It worked—she got the job.

Thank-you notes can be influential, so make certain your letters are mailed immediately after the interview and no longer than 24 hours after you've left the employer. For more advice on excelling in your next inter-view, I recommend you read my book *24 Hours to Your Next Job, Raise, or Promotion* (Wiley).

Thank-You Note Card   I suggest you select a note card with a very professional, businesslike look to use to write this note. If your cursive writing is not clear and legible, then print.

Dear Tom:

Thank you for meeting with me today.
I'm very interested in your Director Position.
I believe my strengths in budgets, planning and fundraising would be an asset to you.

In the past, I've always given 110% and feel that I could again make valuable contributions as the Director of your Association's chapter.

Both your time and consideration are most appreciated.

Mary Brown

Thank-You Letter

Kenneth Smith
1 Cherry Park Lane
Newark, NJ 07081
(201) 555-0111

July 30, 1997

John Zollman
Division manager
Quantron
P.O. Box 67000
Newark, NJ 07088

Dear John:

I found yesterday's meeting both helpful and exciting. The products you are developing, plus the reengineering process you are in the middle of, are a perfect match for my operations and management background.

I pride myself in producing cohesive teams, building morale and achieving the turnaround results you desire. I know I'd make a valuable addition to Quantron. I thank you for the opportunity to learn more about your company.

I await your decision with great interest.

Sincerely,

Kenneth Smith

Kenneth Smith

Kristin Andersen
1575 Hampton Blvd SE
St. Louis, MO 63105
(314) 555-0111

July 27, 1997

Edward Phelps
St. Louis Energy
PO Box 10004
St. Louis, MO 63111

Dear Ed:

Thank you for the opportunity to interview with you today. My only regret is that we had such a short time to discuss the position. So, let me summarize for you the strengths and the skills I would bring to the job and how I would complement the team:

- Extensive project management and budget experience bring projects in on time and within budget.
- Thorough knowledge in gas policies, procedures, construction, safety practices and energy distribution designs.
- Skilled at communicating and working with a diverse group of people in building a productive team and achieving goals while being customer focused.
- Flexible to respond quickly and solve problems when matters need immediate attention.
- Proficient on computer software programs: Project Manager, Cost Estimating/ Materials, Project Scheduling, Windows 95, and Excel.
- Skilled at time management, planning, and prioritizing projects.

If you have any questions, I encourage you to contact me. I want to assure you that I am very interested in the Project Manager position. If you select me, be assured I will give 150% to the job as I always have done.

Your time and consideration are most appreciated.

Sincerely,

Kristin Andersen

Kristin Andersen

Kristin got the job and a significant raise, too!

WRITING SELF-MARKETING LETTERS

7

As you learned in the last chapter, Prospect and Informational Interview letters are a secret weapon that taps into the hidden job market. I've created the basic skeleton or template for each of these letters. They are not difficult letters to write. You can use this template to create your own Prospect and Informational Interview letters.

Prospect Letters

Create a letterhead as follows:

Name
Address
Phone number

Next, write the *opening sentence.* Use a summary of your background and skills in the lead-in. A program manager might write the following:

Ten years coordinating all aspects of workflow, employee supervision, project management and budgets for a nonprofit institution briefly summarizes my background. I've had a proven track record of successfully containing costs while increasing our department's productivity. My strengths include strategic planning, finance, program development and strong communication skills.

Now write your opening sentence:

_____

_____

_____

_____

_____

_____

_____

_____

_____

Now for the pitch: Here's where you'll tell them you'll call them.

I'll call you next week to learn more about your current needs and to further discuss the valuable contributions I would make as part of your team.

The program manager concluded with the following:

Your time and attention are most appreciated.

Sincerely,

His Name

His name

Enclosures: Resumé

Now put it all together and you've created a first-rate letter. Here's what our program manager's letter looks like:

Bob Jones
1 Main Street
City, NY 11111
(201) 555-0111

September 21, 1997

Kerry Brown
ABC Manufacturer
BOX 33333
Dallas, TX 44444

Dear Kerry:

Ten years coordinating all aspects of workflow, employee supervision, project management and budgets for a nonprofit institution briefly summarizes my background. I've had a proven track record of successfully containing costs while increasing our department's productivity. My strengths include: strategic planning, finance, program development and strong communication skills.

I'll call you next week to learn more about your current needs and to further discuss the valuable contributions I would make as part of your team.

Your time and attention are most appreciated.

Sincerely,

Bob Jones

Bob Jones

Enclosures: Resumé

Now it's your turn.

Opening:

_____

_____

_____

_____

Your pitch:

_____

_____

_____

_____

Closing:

Your time and attention are most appreciated.

Sincerely,

Your Name

Your Name

Enclosures: Resumé

You've done it! Mail your letter to a few employers every week and be sure to make that follow-up phone call seven to ten days after it has been mailed.

WHEN YOU HAVE A REFERRAL

Most people use a similar letter, adapting it to reflect any referrals or insider information in the opening sentence.

The program manager might begin as follows:

> Tom Austin mentioned that you may have some need for a good Program Manager. With ten years in the field, and a proven track record of handling both program development and cost containment while increasing productivity, Tom felt a meeting might be to both our benefit. I'll contact you next week. . . .

As you can see, we used the referral's name first to stand out and share the learned information. We also included the major aspects that the contact, Tom, mentioned to us—program development and cost containment. We assume that the employer will talk to us, so we simply state when we'll call and, of course, enclose a resumé with the letter.

The final result looks like this:

Bob Jones
1 Main Street
City, NY 11111
(201) 555-0111

September 21, 1997

Kerry Brown
ABC Manufacturer
BOX 33333
Dallas, TX 44444

Dear Kerry,

Tom Austin mentioned that you may have some need for a good Program Manager. With ten years in the field, and a proven track record of handling both program development and cost containment while increasing productivity, Tom felt a meeting might be to both our benefit. I'll contact you next week to learn more about your current needs and to further discuss the valuable contributions I would make as part of your team.

Your time and attention are most appreciated.

Sincerely,

Bob Jones

Bob Jones

Enclosures: Resumé

These letters are most effective when they are short and to the point. Now write yours by starting out using the *referral's name* and some *important skills and experience* you have to offer.

Your name
Address
Phone number

(Referral's name) _____

_____

_____

_____

_____

_____

I'll contact you next week to learn more about your current needs and to further discuss the valuable contributions I would make as part of your team.

Your time and attention are most appreciated.

Sincerely,

Your Name

Your name

Enclosures: Resumé

Mail your letters out today! These really work in uncovering terrific job opportunities that might just lead to your next position.

Informational Interview Letters

Create a letterhead as follows:

Name
Address
Phone number

Use a referral whenever possible in the *opening sentence* since that gathers the most attention. Then include a brief summary of your background and skills in the first paragraph.

Our program manager might write the following:

Tom Austin mentioned that you would be in an excellent spot to offer me some needed advice.

Now write your opening sentence:

_____

_____

_____

_____

_____

Continue with a brief statement about your background. Our program manager might continue as follows:

As a Program Manager, I have ten years in the field and a proven track record of handling both program development and cost containment while increasing productivity.

Now write your background:

_____

_____

_____

It's time to make your request. I suggest you reassure people about your objective and limit the meeting time you request to 15 to 20 minutes. This makes it easier to grant your request. Bob, our program manager, said:

Tom felt you might be able to offer me some guidance on my current job search. Let me reassure you that I don't expect you to have or even know about a position, but it's a challenging job market right now and Tom thought you might indeed prove quite helpful. I'll contact you next week to arrange a short 15-minute meeting.

Now it's your turn. Make your request:

_____

_____

_____

_____

_____

_____

_____

You've done it! Be sure to follow up and call shortly after this letter's sent. It's always a good idea to write out some questions and your top five selling points to aid you when you finally do get to talk to this employer.

THE EASY TRACKING SYSTEM

8

Find your limits.
Exceed them.
Repeat.
                                    —ROBIN RYAN

During the course of your job search, you'll need to keep records of the date, location, and destination of your letters. I've found that having a single list of all letters sent allows you to trace your progress, as well as to keep track of any follow-up activities that need to be done. Use the Cover Letter Tracking System to record every letter you send out.

BONUS

Efficient, Time-Saving Charts to Use

COVER LETTER TRACKING SYSTEM

Job Applied For	Company	Date Sent	Response	Follow-up Done

The next chart allows you to organize your weekly activities. It's great for planning ahead and making sure you stay on top of your follow-up activities. Be sure to include any names, phone numbers, or addresses for easy execution of the activities.

WEEKLY TO-DO LIST

Want ads to respond to:

_____

_____

Follow-up activities:

_____

_____

Informational Interviews to conduct:

_____

_____

Informational Interviews to arrange:

_____

_____

Self-Marketing/Prospect Letters to send:

_____

_____

Networking events to attend:

_____

_____

Days and times to conduct this work:

_____

_____

_____

Send thank-you notes (*list name and address*):

_____

_____

_____

Hot Leads

Inevitably you'll get hot leads (e.g., "I may have an opening next month—call then"). This requires special follow-up. Use index cards or forms to record the important information.

HOT LEAD

Call on _____ (date)	
Name:	
Company:	
Address:	
Phone:	
E mail:	
Important notes:	
Action to be taken:	

Organize these every week by *date,* so you'll never miss a potential opportunity that might just turn out to be your perfect job.

High-Impact Words and Phrases

These lists will help you select just the right descriptive verb or task to emphasize your strengths to an employer.

Review the lists and check off any appropriate words or tasks you'd like to incorporate into your letter.

Words with Impact

PEOPLE	THINGS	IDEAS
___ Accomplished	___ Built	___ Adapted
___ Activated	___ Calculated	___ Analyzed
___ Adapted	___ Changed	___ Authored
___ Adjusted	___ Compiled	___ Coordinated
___ Administered	___ Completed	___ Created
___ Advertised	___ Constructed	___ Defined
___ Advised	___ Created	___ Devised
___ Analyzed	___ Designed	___ Educated
___ Arranged	___ Drafted	___ Established
___ Assembled	___ Edited	___ Executed
___ Assisted	___ Enlarged	___ Explained
___ Calculated	___ Established	___ Illustrated
___ Cataloged	___ Evaluated	___ Implemented
___ Chaired	___ Examined	___ Initiated
___ Collaborated	___ Expanded	___ Innovated
___ Conceptualized	___ Expedited	___ Integrated
___ Conciliated	___ Fabricated	___ Interviewed
___ Conducted	___ Facilitated	___ Investigated
___ Consulted	___ Familiarized	___ Maintained
___ Contracted	___ Formulated	___ Manipulated
___ Coordinated	___ Generated	___ Marketed
___ Delegated	___ Governed	___ Modified
___ Demonstrated	___ Guided	___ Monitored
___ Developed	___ Hired	___ Negotiated
___ Directed	___ Identified /	___ Obtained
___ Distributed	___ Improved	___ Persuaded
___ Effected	___ Increased	___ Presented
___ Explained	___ Indexed	___ Presided
___ Indoctrinated	___ Influenced	___ Processed
___ Instructed	___ Informed	___ Proposed
___ Interviewed	___ Invented	___ Produced
___ Managed	___ Investigated	___ Publicized
___ Motivated	___ Operated	___ Recommended
___ Negotiated	___ Prepared	___ Recorded
___ Organized	___ Programmed	___ Recruited
___ Programmed	___ Revised	___ Related
___ Promoted	___ Specified	___ Surveyed
___ Stimulated	___ Summarized	___ Synthesized
___ Supervised	___ Used	___ Transmitted

Notable Abilities

You perform many tasks on your job that are important to point out in your letter. Here are some to get you thinking about the major skills you'll bring to an employer.

___ Account Management	___ Accounting	___ Administration
___ Advertising	___ Analysis & Evaluation	___ Budgets
___ Business Management	___ Client Services	___ Computer Programming
___ Computer Skills	___ Consulting	___ Contract Negotiations
___ Counseling/Coaching/ Advising	___ Curriculum Development	___ Customer Service
___ Data Entry	___ Editing	___ Employee Relations
___ Engineering	___ Field Research	___ Financial Analysis
___ Financial Planning	___ Fiscal Management	___ Forecasting
___ Fundraising	___ Graphic Design	___ Hiring
___ Human Resources	___ Inspection	___ Interviewing
___ Inventory Control	___ Investigation/ Research	___ Labor Relations
___ Language Interpretation	___ Market Research	___ Marketing
___ Media Relations	___ Merchandising	___ Multimedia
___ Negotiations	___ Office Administration	___ Outreach
___ Policymaking	___ Presentations	___ Print Coordination
___ Process Improvement	___ Product Development	___ Product Management
___ Production	___ Program Design	___ Program Management
___ Project Management	___ Project Management	___ Promotion
___ Public Relations	___ Public Speaking	___ Publicity
___ Publishing	___ Purchasing	___ Quality Assurance
___ Quality Assurance	___ Quality Improvement	___ Real Estate
___ Records Management	___ Recruiting	___ Reengineering
___ Reporting	___ Research & Development	___ Restaurant Management
___ Retail	___ Sales	___ Statistical Analysis
___ Strategic Planning	___ Strong Communi- cations Skills	___ Supervision
___ Systems Analysis	___ Teaching	___ Technical Skills
___ Technical Writing	___ Telecommunications	___ Testing
___ Training	___ Word Processing	___ Writing

Guidelines to Follow
When You Have a Full-Time Job

Bob Holman, senior trainer for Franklin Quest, who's taught over 700 seminars on Time Management points out: " 'I don't have time to job hunt' is a bogus excuse. You will find time if it's important to you. Every person has the same amount of time—you control your schedule. If you see the need and it has high enough value to you, you'll do it."

Planning your time is essential. I recommend you devote at least *five* hours a week to your job search. This means you must prioritize your time and really screen out potential opportunities. Bob recommends you block out time on your calendar for the job search activities to accomplish. Put them on your weekly to-do list. Thirty minutes to one hour are the easiest amounts of time to carve out of a busy schedule. Plan the tasks. Do the work and write down your progress and any follow-up activities. Another time-saver that Bob suggests is to put complete information on your weekly to-do list—full names, phone numbers, e-mails, or addresses—whatever you'll need so you won't have to waste 15 minutes locating that essential information.

Some self-selection and screening is essential to maximize the effectiveness of the efforts you make. Apply only for the good positions where your qualifications are a strong fit. Try to arrange at least one informational interview per week. Your targeted letters are going to be a major part of your job hunting process, so write and follow up with at least one every week.

After 20 weeks, you will have approached 20 potential employers. Most employed people drag out their job hunts for a year or two. They become disheartened when the first 10 resumés don't land a terrific new job. Job hunting takes concentrated, determined effort. My clients and seminar participants have followed these job hunting guidelines and succeeded in landing great jobs quickly. Don't get discouraged and stop. It's the continuous efforts that bring results. Make your action plan, and implement the strategies you've learned in this book and you, too, will be a success story.

Guidelines to Follow When You're Not Working

If you think you are unemployed, you are very wrong. Now your "job" is looking for a new position. After advising thousands of clients, I find that you'll need to devote 25 to 30 hours per week to your job search plus an additional five hours per week to exercise. When you're unemployed, your self-confidence is usually lower. It's not uncommon to become depressed and lethargic. You may feel it's hopeless. *It's not!* Keeping a positive attitude requires effort. First and foremost, exercise Monday through Friday. Start your day no later than 8:00 A.M., walk, do aerobics, or go to the gym for a workout. Exercise will lift your spirits and allow you to stay on track. It's also a good idea to read motivational books and see movies with happy endings—avoid all the tear-jerkers and depressing stories while you job hunt.

Spending 25 to 30 hours a week on your job search may sound like a lot. Here's how a typical week breaks down: Answer want ads, make follow-up calls, conduct market research to identify prospective companies, and network. Conduct two or three informational interviews. Send out three to four self-marketing letters. Make follow-up calls to employers who received your letters the week before. Keep calling until you reach your contact. (It's best if you call that person because return calls can catch you off guard and ruin the chance to get job leads and information.) Attend one or two association, club, or group meetings to continue networking efforts. Keep accurate records and plan out your upcoming week on Sunday, so that Monday morning you're engrossed in the job hunt again.

BE A SUCCESS STORY

"One of the worst mistakes job hunters make," says HR manager Linda, "is that they simply send a resumé without a cover letter." Throughout our hiring survey many employers echoed this same thought. The final consensus is this: A well-written cover letter is *as important as your resumé* to most hiring managers. Employers told us exactly how best to impress them. Here's what they said:

"Tell me the specific skills you have to offer that fit with what you know about my company's needs."   —*CEO*

"Offer some characteristics that make you valuable to me."   —*Executive VP*

"Relate your background and skills to the job you are applying for."   —*HR manager*

"I notice the overall appearance and if the letter is intelligently written."   —*Senior executive*

"Don't oversell with a lot of puffed-up statements or try to second-guess me by saying, 'I'm sure I'm the best person for the job.' That's for me to decide. Give me facts on how you can do my job."   —*Senior executive*

"Well thought out; personalized to our needs; not a form letter."   —*HR manager*

"Tell me quickly and clearly why I should hire you."
                                          —*HR manager*

"Tell me why I should hire you." several wrote. That's exactly why I developed The Power Impact Technique. I wanted to write cover letters that got employers' attention and answered that very question. A dozen years ago, I developed this technique to help myself get a job. It worked very well for me, even though the competition was steep. I started showing it to friends and students, and the technique was effective for them, too. Since that time, I've taught thousands how to write better cover letters by quickly addressing the employer's needs. Every client in this book (plus hundreds of others who aren't mentioned) has found a new job using the letters and the job hunting techniques I've discussed, explained, and illustrated in *Winning Cover Letters.*

I base my advice on solid research. We surveyed 600 hiring managers from various fields, including CEOs, vice presidents, and human resource managers. These people make decisions every day on whether or not to hire *you.*

I get so much personal satisfaction when I get a letter or phone call saying, "I got the interview." When I know I've helped someone realize his or her own value and clearly communicate that to an employer, it makes my day. And, as so often happens, my clients contact me a few weeks later to ecstatically report, "I got the job!" That's what I live for—to help people find better jobs. *I believe you deserve to get up every morning to go to a job you'll love!* On average, you'll work 11,000 days (nearly 100,000 hours). Don't you want to use all that time in a situation you find personally satisfying? Meaningful employment, I believe, is something we should all strive for. I wrote this book for one reason and one reason only: I want you to land a great job, one that makes you happy and that you enjoy every day! When you're happy with your work and your company, that feeling spills over into the rest of your life.

CAREER COACH *tip*

"Your success lies just ahead!"

—ROBIN RYAN

So many clients generously helped with this book. I kept hearing, "Your techniques really helped me," and "I got a terrific job using your strategies." Client upon client "won" the job they wanted.

Careers are managed, and like it or not, you control your own destiny. The power to obtain a new job is within your grasp. You are a special and unique person whose talents some employer is hoping for. There is an employer—or several employers—out there right now hoping to find someone like you to do that employer's job. Don't keep them waiting. Use The Power Impact Technique. Write letters that cause employers to notice you and want to talk to you. Believe in yourself. I believe in your success. All you have to do is to try, and continue trying, until you land the job of your dreams. You can do it! Just like so many others I've known. Don't let a little fear or rejection stop you. An employer is out there waiting to hire *you.*

About the Author

One of the nation's foremost authorities on job search and hiring, Robin Ryan is the nationally acclaimed and best-selling author of five books: *24 Hours to Your Next Job, Raise, or Promotion; Winning Resumés; Job Search Organizer; Winning Cover Letters;* and *60 Seconds & You're Hired!*

Robin Ryan has appeared on over 400 TV and radio programs, including *NBC Nightly News with Tom Brokaw* and *Oprah.* She's a frequent commentator on the national CNBC television network and is a regular feature on Seattle's KIRO-TV News and KOMO Radio.

A frequent contributor to national magazines and trade publications, she's been featured in *Money, Newsweek, McCall's, Glamour, Good Housekeeping, Cosmopolitan, National Business Employment Weekly, Black Enterprise, Today's Careers, Journal of Accountancy,* and *Executive Strategies,* to name a few. She's appeared on the pages of most major newspapers, including the *Wall Street Journal, Los Angeles Times,* and *Chicago Tribune.* In addition, she writes a job search/career column for the *Seattle Times.*

A licensed vocational counselor for 18 years, Robin Ryan has a private career counseling and resumé writing practice in Seattle. She holds a master's degree in Counseling and Education from Suffolk University, a bachelor's degree from Boston College, and is formerly Director of Counseling Services at the University of Washington.

A popular national speaker, she frequently gives motivational keynotes or seminar programs at conferences, association meetings, and colleges. You can reach her at (425) 226-0414 to inquire about speaking engagements or individual consulting services.